THE FILMS OF
MARLON BRANDO

THE FILMS OF
MARLON

BRANDO

by Tony Thomas

THE CITADEL PRESS

Secaucus, New Jersey

First edition
Copyright © 1973 by Tony Thomas
All rights reserved
Published by Citadel Press
A division of Lyle Stuart, Inc.
120 Enterprise Ave., Secaucus, N.J. 07094
In Canada: George J. McLeod Limited
73 Bathurst St., Toronto 2B, Ontario
Manufactured in the United States of America by
Halliday Lithograph Corp., West Hanover, Mass.
Designed by A. Christopher Simon
Library of Congress catalog card number: 72–95417
ISBN 0–8065–0370–X

ACKNOWLEDGMENTS

I am grateful to a number of people for assitance in putting this book together. Most of the research was done at the library of The Academy of Motion Picture Arts and Sciences in Los Angeles, for which I thank Mildred Simpson and her staff, and at The Ontario Film Institute in Toronto, thanks to Gerald Pratley and his staff. For aid in collecting the illustrations I readily acknowledge the help of Paula Klaw of *Movie Star News* (New York), Oliver Dernberger of Cherokee Books (Hollywood), The Larry Edmonds Bookstore (Hollywood), Rudy Behlmer, Diane Good-rich, John Lebold, Gunnard Nelson, Aldo Maggiorotti of Warner Bros. (Toronto), Duane Morton, Richard Brooke, Glenn Hunter, and Universal Pictures. My thanks, also, to *Newseek* for permitting me to use a portion of Paul D. Zimmerman's article on Marlon Brando, and especially to Pauline Kael who kindly let me use part of her Brando chapter from *Kiss Kiss, Bang Bang* (Little, Brown and Company) and a lengthy quote from her review of *Last Tango in Paris* in *The New Yorker*.

CONTENTS

THE FILMS OF MARLON BRANDO

Brando at twenty-five, just prior to his Hollywood career

BRANDO:
A View by Pauline Kael

Brando represented a reaction against the post-war mania for security. As a protagonist, the Brando of the early fifties had no code, only his instincts. He was a development from the gangster leader and the outlaw. He was antisocial because he knew society was crap; he was a hero to youth because he was strong enough not to take the crap. (In England it was thought that *The Wild One* would incite adolescents to violence.)

There was a sense of excitement, of danger in his presence, but perhaps his special appeal was in a kind of simple conceit, the conceit of tough kids. There was humor in it—swagger and arrogance that were vain and childish, and somehow seemed very American. He was explosively dangerous without being "serious" in the sense of having ideas. There was no theory, no cant in his leadership. He didn't care about social problems or a job or respectability, and because he didn't care he was a big man; for what is less attractive, what makes a man smaller, than his worrying about his status? Brando represented a contemporary version of the free American.

Because he had no code, except an aesthetic one—a commitment to a *style* of life—he was easily betrayed by those he trusted. There he was, the new primitive, a Byronic Dead End Kid, with his quality of vulnerability. His acting was so physical—so exploratory, tentative, wary—that we could sense with him, feel him pull back at the slightest hint of rebuff. We in the audience felt protective: we knew how lonely he must be in his assertiveness. Who even in hell wants to be an outsider? And he was no intellectual who could rationalize it, learn how to accept it, to live with it. He could only feel it, act it out, be *The Wild One* and God knows how many kids felt, "That's the story of my life."

From *Kiss Kiss Bang Bang* by Pauline Kael, published by Little, Brown and Company, Boston, 1968. Reprinted with the permission of the publisher.

Brando played variations on rebel themes: from the lowbrow, disturbingly inarticulate brute, Stanley Kowalski, with his suggestion of violence waiting behind the slurred speech, the sullen face, to his Orpheus standing before the judge in the opening scene of *The Fugitive Kind*, unearthly, mythic, the rebel as artist, showing classic possibilities he was never to realize (or has not yet realized).

He was our angry young man—the delinquent, the tough, the rebel—who stood at the center of our common experience. When, as Terry Malloy in *On the Waterfront,* he said to his brother, "Oh Charlie, oh Charlie . . . you don't understand. I could have had class. I could have been a contender. I could have been somebody, instead of a bum—which is what I am," he spoke for all our failed hopes. It was the great American lament, of Broadway, of Hollywood, as well as the docks.

With Eva Marie Saint in *On the Waterfront*

With director Sidney Lumet in 1959 while making *The Fugitive Kind*

On the evening of December 3rd, 1947, just before the curtain rose on the opening performance of "A Streetcar Named Desire" at the Ethel Barrymore Theatre in New York, Marlon Brando received a telegram from the author of the play:

RIDE OUT BOY AND SEND IT SOLID. FROM THE GREASY POLACK YOU WILL SOME DAY ARRIVE AT THE GLOOMY DANE. FOR YOU HAVE SOMETHING THAT MAKES THE THEATRE A WORLD OF GREAT POSSIBILITIES. EVER GRATEFULLY. TENNESSEE WILLIAMS.

Brando has never played Hamlet and it seems unlikely he ever will. Despite his success and his fame, and wide recognition as a *great actor*, Brando has shown little enjoyment in his ability to act. More often than not he has deprecated the craft of acting, claiming it as a talent within the range of almost every human and minimizing his own achievements on the stage and on the screen: "This business of being a successful actor. What's the point if it doesn't evolve into anything. All right, you're a success. You're accepted, welcomed everywhere. But that's all there is to it."

Marlon Brando's opinions run counter to those of his admirers. He has, as Shakespeare put it, had fame thrust upon him, and unlike almost all other actors, the gift has made him uncomfortable in the attention it has brought him. For most of his life Brando appears to have been *at odds* with the world, and perhaps with himself. He was a lonely boy who grew into a solitary man, withdrawn and brooding, seemingly unfriendly and yet, as Elia Kazan observes, "He is one of the gentlest people I've ever known. Possibly the gentlest." Brando has refused to play the role of superstar, although he is precisely that. He

MARLON BRANDO
Impressions of a Chameleon

loathes publicity and generally avoids interviews with the press, and on those occasions when it has been necessary for him to talk to reporters he has flatly refused to discuss any area of his private life. He is, however, loquacious on the issues that interest him, particularly American civil rights movements, and interviewers have found him well informed on politics, psychiatry, and Eastern philosophy.

Marlon Brando is a paradox, a strange, convoluted man whose behavior has been contradictory, ranging from rudeness and arrogance to great kindness and consideration. Few people claim to know him well but his friends explain him as a man who hides his sensitivity behind a mask of sullenness. They maintain that he is an amusing man with a deadpan wit, highly intuitive and deeply disconcerting to talk to because he has a sixth sense about exposing the motives of those who talk to him. Brando is also a gifted mimic who can physically and vocally imitate most of the people he meets. And for a man who claims no love of acting, it is often said of Brando that "his whole life is an act, he never stops acting."

Part of the paradox of Marlon Brando is that his great fame is built upon very few successes. He has, in fact, enjoyed much less success that most actors of his caliber and he has survived an unusual number of box office failures. His esteem a stage actor is based on just one performance, as Stanley Kowalski in "A Streetcar Named Desire," and immediately after making that impact he deserted Broadway for Hollywood and never returned. Since his arrival in Hollywood in 1949—he was then twenty-five—Brando has appeared on the stage only once, at a summer theatre in Matunuck, Rhode Island, for a few weeks in 1953, playing Major Sergius Saranoff in Shaw's

"Arms and the Man," and states no interest in making any future appearances in the legitimate theatre. As a film star Brando's fame comes from his first six pictures: The Men, A Streetcar Named Desire, Viva Zapata, Julius Caesar, The Wild One, and On the Waterfront. After winning an Oscar for playing a dockworker in Waterfront, Brando surrendered to Hollywood's choice of starring vehicles, such glossy commercial properties as Desirée, Guys and Dolls, The Teahouse of the August Moon, Sayonara, and The Young Lions. They were all modestly successful with the general public yet critics began making rumbles about the wasting of a great talent. In 1958 Brando took over the direction of One-Eyed Jacks, after Stanley Kubrick retreated, and he horrified Paramount by taking more than a year to make the picture and tripling the budget. It was the beginning of a disorientation with the movie moguls, and was soon compounded with Brando's involvement in MGM's lavish re-make of Mutiny on the Bounty. This extremely badly planned project went ten million over budget and the studio executives found Brando a convenient scapegoat.

None of the films Marlon Brando made in the 1960's proved profitable, and several of them were failures artistically as well as commercially. Some, like A Countess from Hong Kong and Candy, were embarrassingly bad. It is difficult to think of another star who has experienced a string of failures as consistent as did Brando in this decade. Critics in this period were constantly writing off Brando, and many admirers came to regret the decline of a man ironically still referred to as "America's finest film actor." Brando contributed to this decline by his own lack of judgment in choosing dubious material, turning down offers of films that proved successful, and

3

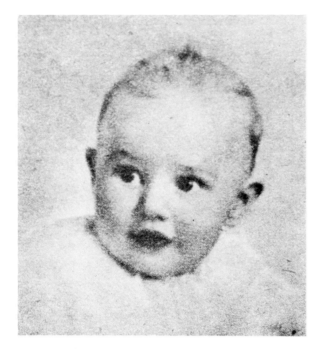

Brando as a baby

Brando at five

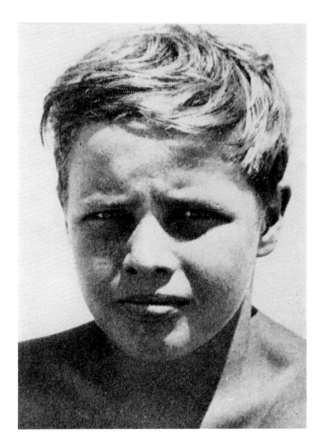

Brando at ten

With sister Frances

4

occasionally being difficult and obdurate with his directors and producers. His behavior was not that of an ambitious star bent on pushing his career. By 1971, Hollywood producers and investors were referring to Brando as box office poison and claiming it was no longer possible to raise money on his name. When producer Al Ruddy and director Francis Ford Coppola suggested to Paramount that Brando play the title role in their production of *The Godfather* they were told to forget the idea and find another actor. Ruddy and Coppola had only two actors in mind, Brando and Sir Laurence Olivier, and when Olivier declined the part for reasons of health, the producer and director took to subterfuge in order to win the role for Brando. They videotaped a screen test with the actor in his home on Mulholland Drive in Beverly Hills, showing a few moments on him made up as Don Vito Corleone. The Paramount executives were greatly impressed with the test although they did not recognize the actor. When told who he was they relented. However, the studio was not willing to pay Brando a large fee; he agreed to $100,000, much less than he had received for most of his films, but asked for,

and received, a percentage of the gross. That contract has subsequently brought him millions.

Marlon Brando's performance as the mafioso chieftain in Mario Puzo's epic story of organized crime in the area of New York City restored him to the prominence he had enjoyed early in his film career. It was a come-back of importance, not a mere returning to favor of a popular player but of a respected actor regaining his stature after years of wavering. Brando now met with the approval of the public, the critics and the manipulators of the movie industry. It was a victory on all fronts. His Don Corleone is a quiet, complex mysterious man with a strict code of conduct and a rigid set of principles. It is a subtle performance full of nuances and small gestures, and to know why Brando was capable of such a characterization requires some understanding of the actor himself. Brando *is* the compassion of Corleone, the sadness, the suspiciousness, the vulnerability and the warmth of the old man. The fact that Corleone is a criminal is beside the point—the point is his devotion to his family and his friends, and his firm adherence to his own set of values. It is not simply his skill that enables

With his mother and Jocelyn

Brando, age thirteen, thumbs his nose at sister Frances. Center is Jocelyn, born 1920, the eldest of the three

Brando to make the old man such a touching and understandable figure, it is the actor's own feelings about the human comedy, so much of which is tragedy, and his own rather tortuous path through life that allows him to reveal the soul of Don Corleone. Meaningful acting requires a knowledge of life, with attendant struggling and suffering, and depth of feeling. The Russian school of acting, led by Stanislavsky, from which the American *method* is largely derived, claims that an actor's success depends upon his own quality as a human being. This appears to be a reasonable explanation for Marlon Brando, an unusually sensitive and observant man with much contempt for the iniquities of life.

Brando has been described in a variety of ways by the people who have worked with him. There are those who dislike him and prefer not to work with him again, claiming that he is disorganized, undisciplined and procrastinating. Others agree that there is some truth in these charges but that Brando's honesty and his intelligence offset them. Several who have known him over the years say that he is a disturbed and troubled man, but the extent of that condition is

known only to the doctors he has consulted and they are duty-bound not to reveal their findings. Some people feel that guilt is a cause of Brando's unrest, guilt stemming from the ease with which he has won fame and huge salaries in a business he has never truly respected. Brando is certainly a peculiar man, and one of the strangest peculiarities of his film life is his seeming desire to indulge in extreme violence in his pictures. Brando is a non-violent man and his friends doubt that he has ever killed or harmed even an insect, and yet he is drawn to any script that includes a savage beating of the character to be played by himself. At the outset of production on *Sayonara* he told director Josh Logan, "I've got to have one brutal scene in every picture." Brando was beaten by a street gang in *Sayonara* and he sustained vicious thrashings in *The Wild One*, *On the Waterfront*, *One-Eyed Jacks*, *The Chase*, and *The Appaloosa*. Several of his other films have contained moments of great physical suffering and the psychiatrists consider this evidence of a Messianic or salvation complex—an atoning of guilt.

In his early years in the theatre in New York

6

Marlon Brando gave wildly inaccurate accounts of his background. The résumés printed in the play-bills of 1944 and 1946 list him as having been born in Calcutta, Bangkok and Rangoon, with bizarre stories about his father being the leader of a zoological expedition. Brando, always given to pranks and practical jokes, looked upon publicity as being absurd and felt that the public had no right to his private life. His attitudes on those points have not changed. Says Brando, "The only thing an actor owes the public is not to bore them." True though this may be, it is a stance that has worked against Brando's quest for privacy, making him more intriguing to the public.

Marlon Brando was born in Omaha, Nebraska, on April 3rd, 1924. His father, Marlon Brando, Sr., was a salesman and later an executive with a company manufacturing insecticides and chemical feed products. Brando was the only son but he had two older sisters, Frances and Jocelyn. His mother, Dorothy Pennebaker (Myers) was an attractive, lively woman who dabbled in amateur dramatics and might, under other circumstances, have become a professional actress. Brando, Sr., was able to provide his family with a comfortable standard of living, although his work required several changes of residence. When Brando, Jr., was six the family moved to Evanston, Illinois, and later to Libertyville, in the same state. The name Brando is derived from French forebears (Brandeau) but both sides of his family are American stock from several generations back. The environment in which Brando grew up has been described as easy-going and Bohemian and somewhat lax in discipline. One friend describes it as the kind of family George S. Kaufman and Moss Hart wrote about in *You Can't Take It With You*. Young Brando was called Bud by his family and his sister Jocelyn recalls him as being a "serious and very determined little boy."

As a child Marlon Brando was mischievous and self-willed, and given to bringing home all manner of objects he gathered by rummaging through garbage piles. His sympathy for underdogs was apparent even at this age and he several times brought home human derelicts including, on one occasion, a drunken woman. He also showed great rapport with animals; the Brando home, on the outskirts of Libertyville, became a menage for stray pets and usually included poultry, dogs, rabbits, a horse, a cow and numerous cats and birds. Brando was so attached to each animal that he objected to any dead cat or bird being bur-

Brando as a cadet at the Shattuck Military Academy at Faribault, Minnesota.

Brando with Ann Shepard in *Truckline Cafe* in New York in 1946

8

ied. One particular chicken to which he was attached was buried and dug up several times.

Brando's record as a scholar was markedly poor. The principal of Libertyville Township High School, H. E. Underbrink, found himself approached years later to repeatedly explain to reporters what the famous actor was like as a schoolboy. Mr. Underbrink chose to be honest and admit that Brando was a problem. "He was rather irresponsible. He wasn't interested in anything in particular. He rarely took part in any extracurricular activities because practically every afternoon he was in our 3:15 P.M. disciplinary period." Brando, Sr., decided that a firm measure had to be taken with his nonconformist son and he enrolled him at the Shattuck Military Academy in Faribault, Minnesota, which he had himself attended.

Marlon Brando was a failure as a military cadet, largely because he had no aptitude for regimentation or protocol. He was sixteen at the time of his enrollment at Shattuck and by then he had already attended a number of schools and been expelled from several. Looking back on his days at the military academy Brando says that he hated every day, especially the strict adherence to a time schedule: "I love the kind of life where time doesn't matter." The academy bell rang every quarter-hour to remind the cadets of their duties and Brando one night climbed the bell tower, removed the clapper and buried it. He recalls that this was a mistake because the academy took to announcing the time with young buglers, whose noise was far worse than the bell. Brando revealed to Pete Martin for an article in *The Saturday Evening Post* that he spent a lot of his time thinking up ways of getting admitted to the academy infirmary: "We didn't have to do any work there, so I feigned illness whenever I could. Once you were in it was hard to get out. Sometimes I was laid up for days with a phony high temperature. When the nurse momentarily turned to other duties, I induced it by rubbing the thermometer against my sheet until the heat of the friction shot the mercury up."

Brando almost completed the course at Shattuck, despite his lack of interest, but he was expelled in the Spring of 1943. His infractions and demerits were many, including emptying chamber pots from windows and wiring electric current to door handles, but the prank that caused his dismissal was his setting off a bomb at a teacher's door. The bomb was made of firecrackers

and Brando poured a trail of hair tonic from the bomb to his room, thinking that the flame would burn away the alcohol and leave no trace. Instead it left a scorched trail along the floor and the culprit was easily traced.

Brando, Sr., was by this time exasperated with his son and somewhat at a loss as to the boy's future. He arranged a job for him as a laborer with a construction company draining farmland and laying tiles in ditches. Brando quit the dull, dirty job after six weeks and took off for New York, where both his sisters were then living. He stayed with Frances, an art student, and also sought advice from Jocelyn, who was studying drama. Brando had appeared in school plays but had given no thought to becoming an actor. His father, at this point, offered to finance Brando in any profession he might choose to study, and for lack of any other leaning Brando chose drama. He claims that it was a casual, almost indifferent choice, arrived at mostly out of respect for his father's concern. Now nineteen, Brando would have been eligible for military service except that he had injured a knee playing football at Shattuck and received a 4F medical rating. In the fall of 1943 Brando entered the Dramatic Workshop of the New School for Social Research. He spent a year at the school, being directed by Erwin Piscator and coming under the influence of Stella Adler, the most distinguished drama coach in America. Shortly after meeting Brando and watching him work Miss Adler remarked to her director husband, Harold Clurman, "In a year this puppy will be the best young actor in the American theatre."

Marlon Brando first appeared on a New York stage in April of 1944, playing two small parts in Stanley Kauffmann's *Bobino* at the Adelphia Theatre. This was a presentation of The American Theatre for Young Folks. A month later he was in their production of "Hannele's Way to Heaven" by Gerhart Hauptmann, again playing two roles, that of a schoolteacher and then an angel in a dream sequence. He also played in Shakespeare's "Twelfth Night" and adaptations of two plays of Molière. All the plays were directed by Erwin Piscator. Drama critics began to make comment on Brando's work and after leaving the school he was able to get a job with the Sayville, New York, Summer Theatre. He played a number of parts, in addition to performing the various backstage chores of a student actor, and at the end of the season he returned to New York to

As Nels in *I Remember Mama* in New York in 1944, with Mady Christians as Mama

look for work in the professional theatre. Through the influence of Maynard Morris, an agent who had been impressed by his student work, he was auditioned by Rodgers and Hammerstein for their presentation of "I Remember Mama," a play written by John Van Druten and about to be directed by him. Brando, never a good "reader," failed to impress Rodgers and Hammerstein and they would have passed him over but for the insistence of Van Druten that the young actor had a special quality. Van Druten hired Brando to play Nels, the fifteen-year-old son of Mama, played in this performance by Mady Christians. The play opened at The Music Box Theatre on October 19, 1944, and received warm notices from most of the critics, several of whom mentioned Brando and noted that he played the part with charm. "I Remember Mama" proved a hit with the theatre-going public and Brando had his first taste of success. His performance as Nels was gentle and pleasant, and only a person knowledgeable about acting could fully appreciate his work in this play. Such a person is director Robert Lewis, who recalls, "When I saw him in "I Remember Mama," he

was so real I didn't think he was acting. I thought he was a boy they had hired to walk on the stage and be himself."

Another person who was greatly impressed with Brando at this time was Edith Van Cleve, a theatrical agent with the Music Corporation of America. Brando showed no interest in her offer to represent him but after several weeks of badgering he relented and signed with MCA. He told Miss Van Cleve to reject any offers from Hollywood and asked her only to protect him from producers and other agents. Brando at this time in his life was not optimistic about his future as an actor and displayed no confidence in himself. Had it not been for the persistence of Edith Van Cleve and the encouragement of Stella Adler he might have drifted away from the theatre. Brando did, in fact, drift through most of 1945, continuing to study acting but also doing odd jobs and some traveling. He did not appear on Broadway again until February 27th, 1946, playing a leading role in Maxwell Anderson's play "Truckline Café."

"Truckline Café" is generally referred to in the annals of the American theatre as the worst play

10

written by Anderson. The New York critics were without mercy in damning it and the play closed after only a few performances. However, it did bring Brando to the fore again and every critic commented favorably on his performance as Sage McRae, a Second World War veteran who returns home to the sad situation of a faithless young wife, whom he kills. The play was produced by Elia Kazan, who was so unimpressed with Brando's audition that he suggested to director Harold Clurman that they forget about using him. Mrs. Clurman (Stella Adler) felt otherwise and persuaded her husband to keep Brando. Kazan's objection was mostly based on Brando's lack of diction and a mumbled intoning of his lines. Clurman decided the best way to improve Brando's vocal projection was to make him mad; he had Brando read his lines while the other actors were taking a break, constantly interrupting him to say he couldn't hear. He yelled at Brando to shout his lines, then to climb a rope screaming his lines, and then to roll across the stage screaming his lines. As Brando rolled Clurman came on to the stage and kicked him, commanding him to speak louder. The shy actor gradually worked himself into a rage and might have become violent had not Clurman then called back the cast and resumed the rehearsal. The experience cured Brando of swallowing his lines and Kazan changed his opinion when he heard the young actor's now audible performance. It was the beginning of a great association, and Kazan was soon among the group of admirers most interested in furthering Brando's career.

The Anderson play, staged at the Belasco Theatre, also brought Brando into contact for the time with Karl Malden. "Truckline Café," set in a cheap diner on the California coastal highway, was a melodramatic parading of some thirty characters, all of them having difficulty adjusting to postwar life. One of them was a drunken sailor and Malden's amusing characterization brought him good notices in this early period of his long career. The play, possibly the first to deal with America's new *lost* generation, also served Brando well. His brooding, pathetic young veteran caught the attention of producer Guthrie McClintic, who offered Brando the part of Eugene Marchbanks in his production of Shaw's "Candida," with Katharine Cornell in the title role. The Shaw play had been staged numerous times since it first appeared in New York in 1903 and the Cornell revival, at the Cort Theatre,

opening on April 4th of 1946, was well received by the critics. The role of Marchbanks, a young poet somewhat based on Shaw himself, is a challenge to any actor and Brando's notices were mixed. Some felt he was inadequate, especially in diction, while a few critics commented on "this fresh interpretation" brightening the production. It was a step forward for Brando and his agent no longer had the problem of getting him in to see producers, although she still had to contend with his shy and frequently gloomy disposition, a demeanor of little help to a fledgling actor.

Brando's next engagement was "A Flag is Born," which opened at the Alvin Theatre on September 5th, 1946. The play by Ben Hecht was a blatant plea to aid the American League for a Free Palestine and it pulled no punches in criticizing Britain's involvement in the Holy Land, and the general indifference of the world to the plight of the Jews. Most of the action was set in a graveyard by the side of a road leading to Palestine, along which two old refugees (Paul Muni and Celia Adler) make their way. They stop in the graveyard to rest and pray, and there meet a bitter, cynical young Jew (Brando) called David, through whose mouth Hecht voiced his concern for his race and his contempt for the rest of mankind. By the end of the play the old couple had persuaded David to join them on their trek and become a freedom fighter for the Palestinian underground, "A Flag Is Born" was considered too propagandistic for its own good but Brando made an impact with his David and the critics marked him as a talent to be watched for in any future assignments.

1946 was an interesting year for the twenty-two-year-old actor, but more than a year would pass before Broadway would see him again. His luck through the first half of 1947 was not good, although much of the lack of it was due to his own strange behavior. His agent arranged auditions and interviews for him but he either failed to impress the potential employers or walked out before getting his turn to perform. He was interviewed by Lunt and Fontanne for their production of "Oh Mistress Mine" and when he got to the theatre he was told to go on the stage and read for the script. Brando was never able to do this, he could only perform material after he had learned it. On this occasion he simply stood on the stage with the script in his hand saying nothing. Mr. Lunt told him it would be all right if he recited any material of his choosing. Brando then mumbled, "Hickory, dickory, dock" and walked off the stage, never looking back at Lunt and Fontanne. Shortly thereafter he was auditioned by Noel Coward for his flippant comedy "Present Laughter." Brando read over some of the lines to himself, threw the script down and said to Coward, "Don't you know there are people in the world starving?" His manner was even less unyielding when an actor friend arranged a screen test for him without telling him. Brando kept the appointment but he arrived with a yo-yo in his hand, which he refused to put down, and he was filmed playing with the yo-yo. Nothing came of the test.

Brando's agent did manage to get him one engagement in the early part of 1947. He was hired to appear opposite Tallulah Bankhead in Jean Cocteau's "The Eagle Has Two Heads," in which he played Stanislaus, a young poet-peasant who comes to assassinate his Queen but instead falls in love with her. The tempestuous Bankhead took a disliking to her unconventional young leading man and he was fired two days before the play was due to open. When this Ruritanian tale of doomed lovers appeared on Broadway, it was Helmut Dantine who played the poet.

When not begrudgingly appearing at auditions Brando spent his time studying yoga, at which he became so proficient he could actually rotate his stomach muscles, and dancing with Katherine Dunham, appearing in some of her exhibitions of experimental dancing. He also perfected his interest in bongo drumming and became good enough to sit in with professional musicians in small cabarets. Some time in the summer of 1947 his agent chanced to read the script of a new play by Tennessee Williams called "A Streetcar Named Desire." She thought Brando would be good for the leading male role and talked it over with Elia Kazan, who had been slated to direct the play. Kazan agreed, although the part of a loud, uncouth, extraverted mechanic named Stanley Kowalski was a great departure fom anything Brando had done so far. Ironically it would become the role with which the actor is most identified, playing it so arrestingly that it has led people to think that perhaps the actor is somewhat like the character invented by Williams. Brando's own mode of dress in these early years, casual and untidy—"a hippie twenty years before his time" as one of his friends puts it—tended to foster the comparison with Kowalski,

A Streetcar Named Desire as staged at the Barrymore Theatre in New York, 1948. Brando holds Kim Hunter at left. Central are Karl Malden, Nick Dennis and Rudy Bond. Jessica Tandy is at far right.

13

Wardrobe testing while making *A Streetcar Named Desire*

although Brando's own personality is the opposite.

Elia Kazan was so convinced of the value of getting Brando for the play that he telephoned Tennessee Williams at his cottage on the beach at Provincetown, Massachusetts, and asked if he could send the young actor to see him. Williams was agreeable and Brando hitchhiked his way from New York to Cape Cod, not having enough money for a bus fare. He arrived at the Williams cottage at daybreak and sat outside until he heard the playwright getting his breakfast a few hours later. Once inside the cottage Brando found Williams distressed because the lights were off and the plumbing in the bathroom was not functioning properly. Brando fixed the lights and the plumbing, and spent the rest of the day with Williams. Sensing that he was tense and nervous Williams allowed a few hours to pass before asking Brando to read aloud passages from the play Williams knew after a few minutes, as he has said many times since, that this was the actor to play Kowalski. He called Kazan to tell him so and he then loaned Brando twenty dollars to get back to New York. Brando soon afterwards went into rehearsals and one of the people who recall meeting him during this period is Truman Capote. Capote happened to arrive at the theatre one afternoon and approached Brando as he was sleeping on top of a table on the stage. He looked, says Capote, like a weight-lifter, except that there was a copy of Sigmund Freud's *Basic Writings* resting on his chest, and his refined, gentle face gave Capote the feeling of belonging to another body. "Not the least suggestion of Williams' unpoetic Kowalski. It was therefore rather an experience to observe, later that afternoon, with what chameleon ease Brando acquired the character's cruel and gaudy colors, how superbly, like a guileful salamander, he slithered into the part, how his own persona evaporated . . ."

"A Streetcar Named Desire" was an immediate success, bringing acclaim to Marlon Brando and his co-stars Jessica Tandy, Kim Hunter and Karl Malden. The public was astounded by Brando's Kowalski, a brutal, unfeeling, ill-mannered slob who pitilessly exposes his neurotic, fantasizing sister-in-law, and forces her into madness. Looking back on Kowalski Brando says he was the kind of man, "so muscle-bound he could hardly talk. Stanley didn't give a damn how he said a thing. His purpose was to convey his idea. He had no awareness of himself at all." It was an ob-

14

servation drawn from life and Brando saw Kowalski as a victim of the industrial age, a rough, primitive working man surviving with his fists and his back. Says one director of Brando's performance in "Streetcar": "It was awful and it was sublime. Only once in a generation do you see such a thing in the theatre."

Stella Adler has frequently been asked to explain the talent of her brilliant student but she refuses to take the credit. "Marlon never really had to learn how to act. He knew. Right from the start he was a universal actor. Nothing human was foreign to him. He had the potential for any role. It's incredible how large the scale of his emotion is—he has complete scale. And he has all the external equipment—looks and voice and power of presence—to go with it. I taught him nothing. I opened up the possibilities of thinking, feeling, experiencing, and as I opened those doors, he walked right through them." Asked to explain Brando on a more personal level, Miss Adler has said: "He lives the life of an actor 24 hours a day. If he is talking to you, he will absorb everything about you—your smile, the way your teeth grow. His style is the perfect marriage of intuition and intelligence."

"A Streetcar Named Desire" ran at the Ethel Barrymore theatre all through 1948 and the first half of 1949. Brando gave some three hundred performances during the first year and began to show signs of being bored and stifled by the repetition of the part. His general manner when not on stage was said to be "moody and unpredictable" and he occasionally shocked people with his bluntness, such as the time during a performance when he walked to the footlights and told a talkative woman in the audience to be quiet. During the early months of this engagement Brando lived in a cluttered two-room attic apartment in New York's genteel old Murray Hill district and he paid $23 a month rent. He was not at this time in his life bothered by living in dingy quarters and those who knew him then say that he was untidy in the extreme. Brando later shared a $65 a month apartment with Wally Cox, then a nightclub comic, until Cox moved out after repeatedly being bitten by Brando's pet raccoon. Brando lived in a number of cheap abodes during his years in New York and whichever tenant followed him had the problem of redirecting girl friends. One solved the problem by hanging a notice on the door: MARLON DOESN'T LIVE HERE ANYMORE.

At the time of appearing in the New York production of "Streetcar" Brando received a salary of $550 a week. Of this he kept $150 and sent the remainder to his father to invest. Brando, Sr., set up a company titled Marsdo, Inc.—arrived at from the words "Marlon's dough"—and put the money into a cattle ranch in Nebraska, Penny Poke, and oil lands in Indiana. Brando, Jr., badly needed financial advice since his habits with money were exceedingly casual and careless. Despite his low rent and his inexpensive life style, and the large slice of his salary he kept for himself, Brando was usually short of cash within a few days of being paid because he gave much of it away and lost a lot through sheer disregard of where he left his money. Brando has never been tight and numerous friends attest to his generosity. He has been known to take off an overcoat during a winter walk in New York and give it an unemployed actor, explaining that he was just on his way to a store to buy another coat. On another occasion, when he was in Hollywood, Brando learned that an acquaintance had been taken ill with bleeding ulcers and unable to pay his hospital bills. Brando immediately flew to New York and took over the situation.

Shortly after "Streetcar" opened, Elia Kazan, along with Cheryl Crawford and Robert Lewis, founded the Actor's Studio, a drama school that was the origin of the so-called method style of acting. Brando joined the school and became its most famous graduate. Among other things he played the role of a Hapsburg prince in "Reunion in Vienna." The Actor's Studio was an experimental workshop for professionals and it had a great impact on American acting in the postwar years. Many famous stage and screen personalities attended classes and received guidance from directors and teachers like Stella Adler and Lee Strasberg. The two people who had the greatest influence on Brando were undoubtedly Miss Adler and Elia Kazan. Brando openly acknowledges this but, for reasons he cannot seem to explain, his closeness with Kazan drifted into an estrangement. Be that as it may, Kazan has never altered his high opinion of Brando. "Some actors are all instinct and emotion—and no intellect. But Marlon has a brain and can use it. He has a very good analytical understanding of a dramatic problem." To anyone who suggests to Kazan that Brando underacts, Kazan replies, "He doesn't underact inside." When interviewers Stuart Byron and Martin L. Rubin discussed Brando for the

At the Brando home in Libertyville, Illinois, in 1950, with Frances, Marlon Brando, Sr., Frances' daughter Julia, and Mrs. Dorothy Brando

With his grandmother, Mrs. Elizabeth Myers, in Los Angeles in 1950, while he was making *The Men*

With Elia Kazan on the set of *A Streetcar Named Desire* at the Warner Bros. studio

16

British publication *Movie*, Kazan told them that his own restrained intensity was much like that of the actor, that he and Brando were both men who held back their love and anger, their feelings and emotions: "That's my own taste, and that's why I like Brando, and that's why I understood him. He's like that—he's full of deep hostilities, longings, feelings of distrust, but his outer front is gentle and nice. That's him. Brando is, in my opinion, the only genius I've ever met in the field of acting. He would constantly come up with ideas that were better than the ones I had. All he'd do was nod. I'd tell him what I wanted, he'd nod, and then he'd go out and do it better than I could have hoped it would be."

By his twenty-fourth birthday, in 1948, Marlon Brando had crossed the line from obscurity into fame. In the minds of the critics and the acting profession he was a success, not only as an actor of remarkable ability but an actor with an unusual charisma. Brando had received offers from film producers before he appeared in "A Streetcar Named Desire" but with his electrifying performance as Stanley Kowalski offers arrived from every studio. He instructed his agent to reject all of them and it was not until after he had finished with the play that he gave consideration to the idea of making a film. He was vacationing in Paris in the summer of 1949 when a representative of Stanley Kramer handed him an outline of a scenario about the postwar problems of paraplegic servicemen. Brando considered this a film worth doing and he signed a contract with Kramer to head the cast of *The Men* for a fee of $40,000. The film was only a modest success with the general public but it proved that Brando's strange magic as a stage actor also came across on film. The New York theatrical community assumed that he would return to the stage but they were wrong. Brando has not, to this date, acted in a Broadway theatre since his final performance in "A Streetcar Named Desire" and for this he has been continually chided by those in his profession who seem to feel it was his obligation to become a great American stage actor. The sentiment has never made much impression on Brando who has frequently said that he has never had any desire to become a classical actor and that acting has brought him little joy. He says, and it is perhaps rather sad to hear such an admission from so gifted an actor, "The things that give me satisfaction are personal, and have nothing to do with my business."

No actor ever arrived in Hollywood with greater contempt for the film colony than Brando. Stanley Kramer advised his associates to avoid the usual ostentatious welcome given a Broadway actor arriving in Hollywood to star in his first film, but even with this warning they were not prepared for the sullen indifference Brando showed to even the basic standards of behavior for public figures. His wardrobe on arrival consisted of one shabby suit and several changes of blue jeans and T-shirts, and he refused to accept the hotel accommodations arranged for him. Instead he proceeded to the home of an aunt and uncle, Mr. and Mrs. Oliver Lindenmayer, in Eagle Rock, a very plain suburb of Los Angeles. The two-bedroom home was also occupied by Brando's grandmother, Mrs. Elizabeth Myers, and the only sleeping space for the actor was a couch in the living room, which he accepted. His untidiness and his slovenly eating habits were a shock to his relatives. They were embarrassed by the visits of reporters and photographers wanting to interview Brando, who was quite willing to be interviewed wearing his grandmother's dressing gown. Brando stayed with the Lindenmeyers while working on *The Men*, except for the two weeks he spent at the Birmingham Veterans Hospital to study the patients. He gave short shrift to Hollywood's famous commentators and told people the only reason he was making a film was that he didn't have the moral courage to reject the money. Brando appeared to be genuinely mystified by the propriety of his relatives and their concern over his irregular habits and his lack of social decorum.

Despite his manners Brando made an impact on Hollywood. It was obvious to the film makers that he was a powerful actor and an arresting personality, and as such he was a marketable commodity. Brando realized that and resisted it, yet also realizing that it was a fact of life impossible to avoid. His resentment took the form of surly behavior and bitter comment on the Hollywood *powers that be*. Brando nonetheless became part of the success syndrome: for his second film, *A Streetcar Named Desire* he received $75,000; for his third, *Viva Zapata!* he received $100,000 with similar increases until he finally earned the sum of one million dollars in 1960 for appearing in *The Fugitive Kind*, a film he did not really want to make. For his work in *Mutiny on the Bounty* Brando earned more than a million

While making *The Wild One*, Brando was visited by his sister Jocelyn, then working in Hollywood for the first time and appearing in *The Big Heat*

Brando, always loathe to conform, gradually came to terms with his success but managed to remain an individual, never succumbing to Hollywood social life or partaking of publicity schemes. He averaged only one film per year, far less than the usual output for a star, and spent a great deal of his time traveling the world. Brando, because of his early behavior in Hollywood, was often referred to as The Slob but he soon dispensed with juvenile clothing and quickly improved his manners, just as he vastly supplemented his education with reading and study. His friends feel that one of his problems was the gap between his lack of formal learning and his considerable intellect. Brando has also received much psychiatric help, beginning as far back as his days as a student actor in New York and continuing through his early years in Hollywood.

Marlon Brando has concealed, as best he can, any discussion of matters pertaining to his private life and his personal affairs, and he also re-

due to the filming far exceeding the time period of his contract. By this time in his career Brando had made enemies in the film industry because of his apparent lack of regard for budgets and schedules, and he also took blame for situations not of his own making. MGM, for example, found it convenient to allow people to assume that their bad handling of *Mutiny on the Bounty* was due to Brando.

While he was making *Desirée* at 20th Century-Fox in 1954 Brando looked back on his first few years in Hollywood and told a *Time* correspondent: "When I first came to Hollywood I had a rather precious and coddled attitude about my own integrity. It was stupid of me to resist so directly the prejudice that money is right. But just because the big shots were nice to me I saw no reason to overlook what they did to others and to ignore the fact that they normally behave with the hostility of ants at a picnic. The marvelous thing about Hollywood is that these people are recognized as sort of the norm, while I am the flip."

Brando with his Oscar for *On the Waterfront* and envious MC Bob Hope

Preparing for his role as Sky Masterson in *Guys and Dolls,*
Brando practices with composer-lyricist Frank Loesser

sists attempts on the part of interviewers to
talk about the art of acting: "The public isn't interested in reading about acting—they'd rather
read about my alleged romances." Brando has,
according to those close to him, indulged in a
great deal of romancing over the years and his
taste in women is marked by an attraction to
dark, exotic ladies. Among the actresses whose
names have been linked with his are Rita Moreno,
Nancy Kwan and France Nuyen. Brando's first
marriage was to Anna Kashfi, who was raised in
India and refers to herself as Indian despite her
British parents. They were married on October
11th, 1957 and separated a year later, with a divorce granted in 1960. The separation and the
subsequent squabbles over the custody of their
son, Christian Devi, were bitter and sometimes
violent, and the publicity given them has been a
source of embarrassment to Brando. After years
of appealing for custody he was finally given
charge of the boy.

With Anna Kashfi in 1957

19

Brando on his 35th birthday, April 3, 1959, while making *One-Eyed Jacks*. With him is Mexican actress Pina Pellicer

With director-producer George Englund in 1963 while making *The Ugly American*

Brando married again on June 4th, 1960. His second wife was Mexican actress Movita Castenada, whose career began when she played a Tahitian girl in the 1935 filming of *Mutiny on the Bounty*. Several years older than Brando, she had been a close friend from his earliest days in Hollywood. They were divorced in July 1968 and unlike the dissolving of his previous marriage, the case was handled quietly and the court records were ordered sealed at the request of both parties. Many people were unaware of the marriage and the closed-door annulment was conducted to protect the two children, Sergio and Rebecca, of Brando and Movita. No details of the settlement were revealed. Brando is also the father of a son born out of wedlock. The mother is Tarita, a Tahitian who appeared opposite Brando in the re-make of *Mutiny on the Bounty*. The boy is named Tehotu and sees his father frequently on Brando's trips to Tahiti, where he owns property. It is Tahiti where Brando will probably settle once his career as an actor is finished.

Brando's sisters, Frances and Jocelyn, and his parents, both deceased (the mother died in 1953 and the father in 1965), respected his demands for privacy and reporters were unable to pry personal revelations from them. Brando let his guard down on only one occasion; he was visited by Truman Capote in Japan while making *Sayonara* and during long hours of late-night conversation with the brilliant author he exposed some of his fears, doubts and regrets, a lack of rapport with his father and his attachment to his mother, whom he said he "worshipped." Brando also discussed his apparent inability to trust anyone enough to be able to love them, "But what else is there? That's all it's all about. To love somebody." All of this was reported in detail in Capote's long article for *New Yorker*,* to Brando's regret and anger.

Asked to explain his dislike for the press, Brando says, "Because writers are irresponsible, cruel, vicious and exploitive. Because my private life is my business. Because I have been made to appear falsely. I am not a roughneck, a slob, a ring-a-ding. I'm a human being. I have no right to ask *you* personal questions. Why, because I'm an actor, have you the right to ask me? It isn't easy in Hollywood. They don't bother asking questions—they write stories anyway. I have no use for columnists. They're detestable and boring. I despise movie magazines. I think it's in-

* *New Yorker:* November 9, 1957.

20

sipid for national publications to pander to the market of such impoverished thinking." Be that as it may, Marlon Brando has come up with no answers to solve the dilemma of the man fate cuts out to be a famous actor—how to be successful, respected and liked, and contend with the interest of the public. Ironically, Brando's protestations have served to make him even more interesting and, as many critics have pointed out, it is the renegade in Brando, even more than his talent, that has made him an appealing figure in an age of conformity and restriction.

Marlon Brando has many times turned down offers to appear in films that later became successful, *Lawrence of Arabia* was one of them, but unlike most actors he has shown little regret and whatever disappointment he has felt over the failure of most of his films in the 1960's he has kept to himself. Early in 1968 he declined an offer from 20th Century–Fox to star in *Butch Cassidy and the Sundance Kid*. More surprisingly he shied away from appearing in *The Arrangement*, which would have reunited him with Elia Kazan after a fourteen-year lapse in their once close association. Despite the great bearing Kazan had on Brando's early career, and the fact that he directed three of the actor's best films, Brando let slide their friendship. Kazan claims that several scripts sent to Brando were returned through Brando's agent, although there was a tentative agreement to do *The Arrangement*, Kazan's own direction and production of his best selling book. Kazan particularly wanted Brando for this convoluted study of an affluent advertising executive cracking under the strain of his personal and business life, and rebelling against the values and standards of his environment. Brando, according to Kazan, made it impossible for Kazan to use him and he then hired Kirk Douglas to play the part. Despite a brilliant performance from Douglas, the film was a conspicuous flop, which is something the intuitive Brando might have sensed from the start. Kazan admits that Douglas in some ways was a better choice for the part, that the actor's own forceful personality better suited the playing of a tough executive. What Kazan wanted from Brando was the ambivalence that he would have brought to the interpretation. In writing a part that largely reflected Kazan's own feelings toward the dilemma of modern life, Kazan wanted to utilize what he describes as Brando's "inner-contradictoriness," something

With his wife Movita, on the evening of November 15, 1962, at the West Coast premiere of *Mutiny on the Bounty*

Brando conga drumming in New York, once one of his favorite hobbies

With director Arthur Penn in 1966 while making *The Chase*

Brando in 1965

he admits to having in common with the actor, and he assumes that Brando avoided *The Arrangement* because he understood the story so well he felt uncomfortable about it—"it was very close to something basic in him."

Brando had little to say about his refusal to appear in *The Arrangement*, except that he was looking for more politically pertinent vehicles: "You can say important things to a lot of people. About discrimination and hatred and prejudice. I want to make pictures that explore the themes current in the world today." Brando had admired Gillo Pontecorvo's *The Battle of Algiers* and told the director he would be interested in working with him. Pontecorvo quickly took advantage of the sentiment and suggested filming a militantly anti-imperialist story about an uprising on a Caribbean island in the mid-19th century. First titled *Quemada*, then changed to the Portuguese spelling of *Queimada* because the Spanish government objected to any aspersion on their involvement in the New World, the film told of European subjugation of a native population for reasons of commerce, and the producers were clearly willing to allow audiences to infer a parallel with Vietnam. The project appealed to Brando and he agreed to the film being shot in the remote location of Cartagena, Colombia. Filming started in the summer of 1968 and then dragged on for month after weary month with a huge crew, a largely amateur cast and the use of thousands of extras. Pontecorvo and Brando soon began to differ on many aspects of production and story concept, and eventually became hostile to one another. By February of 1969 Brando left Colombia and advised Pontecorvo that whatever remained to be filmed would have to be done elsewhere. Pontecorvo had shown no hurry in making the lengthy picture but he had completed about ninety per cent of the footage at the time Brando left. The additional material was shot in Morocco and at European locations, involving the company for almost one year of production, at the end of which time only a handful of the original crew were still on salary. The title of the film was changed to *Burn!* for North American release, with prints running a full twenty minutes short of the European version, and it failed to make much impression on either the critics or the public. Sadly for Marlon Brando, *Burn!* appeared to be yet another in a continuing line of box office disappointments.

At the time Pontecorvo and his company were

With Elizabeth Taylor during a break in the filming of *Reflections in a Golden Eye*

laboring on their picture in Colombia, Paramount had a huge cast and crew only a few miles away working on a multi-million dollar filming of Harold Robbins' *The Adventurers*. This, too, would emerge as a spectacular failure —much more so than *Burn!*—but at the time Paramount spared no expense to promote its product, even flying in a large group of European, American and Canadian journalists. To a man the journalists tried to make their way to the location of the other film in the hope of getting an interview with Marlon Brando. By this time Pontecorvo's publicists had long given up on getting Brando to do anything or see anyone. He refused to make any comment about *Burn!* His quitting of the location coincided with the departure of several of the journalists, and on a flight from Cartagena to Miami, Toronto entertainment reporter Sid Adilman happened to find himself sitting in an aisle seat across from Brando. Recalls Adilman, "I had been watching Brando read and was waiting for an opening. Unwittingly, he provided it, leaning across the aisle to ask, 'Would you happen to have a match?' With the match went an introduction. I was not inetrested in his *personal* life. Very simply, I wondered if we could chat for a while. He nodded his head half-heartedly." Adilman brought up the issue of Brando backing out on Kazan's *The Arrangement* and asked him why. Replied Brando, "I was overcome by the Martin Luther King assassination. I have been concerned lately with man's predatious nature. More and more I feel it is difficult to achieve a rapprochment with oneself and with the fact of man's tendency to behave aggressively." He then borrowed another match, lit another cigarette, refused lunch offered by a stewardess, leaned toward Adilman and asked him if he had total recall. "If not, then take notes so you can make sure to get everything down. I'm very serious about this." Brando went on to discuss his disgust with mankind's aggressiveness and his doubts about the survival of the human species. He spoke of the liquidation of multitudes of people of various races and creeds, and in particular of the treatment of the Indian tribes of America. Speaking in quiet, measured tones Brando told the Canadian writer, "If the world were organized tomorrow in such a way that we were all one color and we all had the same political philosophy and one economic system and we all spoke the same language, the right-handed people would start to find some

way to harass and exterminate all the left-handed people. People have a need for an enemy. They need to find a target and they need to find an evil. The failure of religion has proved that it can't and hasn't taught brotherly love well at all. Madison Avenue is a testament of the fact that anything can be sold—anything I guess except brotherly love."

After going on at some length on these themes Brando began to fidget with a magazine and Adilman astutely put away his notebook. But as the plane was landing in Miami Brando looked across at Adilman and said, "You know, that sounded awfully pompous. I really meant what I said." With that Brando then added his usual jaundiced view of newspaper reporters—that they go away and write whatever they wanted to write before they came. The interview had been on Brando's own terms, discussing only topics of his choice and yet he was still suspicious of the reporter and doubtful that he would be quoted accurately. In talking to other journalists who have interviewed Brando, Adilman assumes the actor is hostile to the press for fear of being asked questions for which he might have no answers, thereby making himself a target. Like the other writers on the Colombian junket, Adilman had tried to talk to Brando on or off the set of *Burn!* but had been denied any access to him. He did, however, get into conversation with one of the technicians on the film, who told him that Brando one evening put to him the question: "If you had ten million dollars and you were unhappy, what would you do?" The technician mused on the thought for a moment and then said to Adilman, "Brando is looking for something. I'm sure of that."

The success of *The Godfather* caused a re-focusing on Marlon Brando. For some years critics and film commentators had lamented the decline of a great talent, the bad luck and the bad judgment in appearing in flop films, with a subsequent loss of prestige and popularity. Says Elia Kazan, "Brando has been good in everything he's done but he was a trapped giant in all those lesser films, and people were always ready to say 'he's had it'." *The Godfather* brought about a change of tune. Critics were eloquent in praising his performance as Don Corleone and the phrase "America's finest actor" once again became part of the language of the entertainment business. The success and the praise seemed to make little difference to Brando's disposition al-

23

though it made a great deal of difference to his financial well being, bringing him in a vast and continuing amount of money that will possibly leave him free of material care for the rest of his life. But reporters, approaching him as if this success may have changed his attitude toward his work, found the imperturbable Brando just as unwilling to wax enthusiastic as before: "It may seem peculiar but I've spent most of my career wondering what I'd really like to do. Of course, I've had to make a living but acting has never been the dominant force in my life."

Conversations with Brando can be exciting and challenging provided they deal with travel, politics, philosophy and books, and if they avoid the theatre and the movies. Brando claims to have given little thought to the direction of his career, taking it as a matter of course and not being concerned with considerations of success or failure. He does admit that there are things he might have done differently. But even with the great upsurge of interest in him and his career fostered by *The Godfather* Brando still speaks of retiring from his profession, as he has for several years, and devoting his time to civil rights, the plight of subjugated races, and to research into ways of discovering new sources of food from ocean plankton at an institute he plans to build on his property in Polynesia. His disdain for being a celebrity remains the same and he occasionally laughs at what he considers the ridiculousness of it all, "As soon as you become an actor, people start asking you questions about politics, astrology, archeology, and birth control. And what's even funnier, you start giving opinions."

The renewed interest in Marlon Brando took on an even greater intensity early in 1973 when the press confirmed rumors that he had made a film involving long, graphic passages of stunningly sexual material. *The Last Tango in Paris* was then given an amazing amount of coverage in the news magazines, more than any film had ever received, creating a controversy even before it was released and touching off widespread discussions on filmed pornography and the relative values and dangers of permissiveness in the cinema. In an apparently totally uninhibited performance Brando chose not to restrain himself in matters of nudity, language and sexual expression. Whether Brando fully realized the completeness of his cooperation with director Bernardo Bertolucci is known only to the actor himself, but he did tell Bertolucci that he felt used and violated and that he would never again make a film of this nature. Certainly the film is revealing in more ways than merely physical, dealing as it does with the anguish of a tormented, middle-aged Midwesterner, who muses on an unhappy childhood, estrangement from his parents and a string of bitter, painful relationships with women. Students of Brando have good reason to consider *The Last Tango in Paris* his most personal picture.

Paul D. Zimmerman, the film critic of *Newsweek*, wrote a lengthy, perceptive essay* on Marlon Brando and ended it with a summation that strikes a sympathetic response in those who take seriously the career of this unusual and valuable actor:

In the end, however, the thoughtful observer must reject Brando's pessimistic and denigrating assessment of his own achievements. Everyone may indeed be an actor. But there is only one Brando. His great performances—Stanley Kowalski in *Streetcar* and Terry Malloy in *Waterfront*—and even many of his lessor ones—broaden our sense of the human condition, stretch our sensibilities, inform our lives. Everyone who has seen him act has been in some way changed by Marlon Brando. Like all great actors, he shows us what it is to be human. His Don Corleone is great not as a monster —although in social terms that is indeed what he is— but because of the dimensions of sympathy and pathos Brando brings to him. It is because of Marlon Brando that we can see something of ourselves even in as forbidding a figure as the Godfather. It is Brando's gift to us.

* *Newsweek*, March 13, 1972. Copyright Newsweek, Inc., 1972, reprinted by permission.

Brando in *The Godfather*

A Stanley Kramer Production, released by United Artists.
Produced by Stanley Kramer.
Associate Producer: George Glass.
Directed by Fred Zinnemann.
Screenplay by Carl Foreman.
Photographed by Robert De Grasse.
Production designed by Rudolph Sternad.
Edited by Harry Gerstad.
Musical score by Dimitri Tiomkin.
Running time: 86 minutes.

CAST:

Ken	Marlon Brando
Ellen	Teresa Wright
Dr. Brock	Everett Sloane
Norm	Jack Webb
Leo	Richard Erdman
Angel	Arthur Jurado
Nurse Robbins	Virginia Farmer
Ellen's Mother	Dorothy Tree
Ellen's Father	Howard St. John
Dolores	Nina Hunter
Laverne	Patricia Joiner
Mr. Doolin	John Miller
Dr. Kameran	Cliff Clark
Man at Bar	Ray Teal
Angel's Mother	Marguerite Martin

Marlon Brando began receiving offers from Hollywood soon after he had established himself in the New York presentation of "A Streetcar Named Desire." He turned all of them down. At one point in 1948 he said, in one of his many snide comments on Hollywood producers, "They've never made an honest picture in their lives and probably never will." The man

THE MEN

(1950)

who called Brando's bluff was Stanley Kramer. Kramer set up his own production company in 1949 and set about making films that had something to say about the vital issues of contemporary life. His first film, *Champion*, was a searing insight into the brutal, corrupt, blood sport of boxing, and he followed it with *Home of the Brave*, the first major American film to face up to the bitterness of racial discrimination. For his third film Kramer chose to deal with the problems of paraplegic veterans in postwar society, something that was considered even less commercial as film fare than his previous pictures. To compound what seemed like folly in the eyes of his fellow producers, Kramer sought a leading man whose name would mean nothing on the marquees of most movie theatres. He sent Brando a synopsis of the script of *The Men* and a few days later received an affirmative reply from the actor.

The screenplay of *The Men* was written by Carl Foreman, who had also scripted *Champion* and *Home of the Brave*, and in order to get the utmost accuracy and feeling into his story Foreman spent much time at the Birmingham Veterans Administration Hospital in Van Nuys, California. To further ensure a tasteful and intelligent treatment Kramer hired the gentlemanly Fred Zinneman as his director. The next step was for Kramer and Zinnemann to persuade Brando to spend some time at the Birmingham hospital to familiarize himself with the nature of his assignment. No persuasion was necessary; within a few days of being in Hollywood Brando suggested that he move to the hospital for a period. He spent a full two weeks there, virtually as a patient, living in a ward, undergoing therapy, using a wheelchair to move himself around and going with the men on their social and recreational activities. Brando was able to persuade the paraplegics, some of whom were at first resentful of the actor and the idea of the film, of the sincerity of the project. Much of the picture was shot at Birmingham and forty-five of the patients agreed to appear in it.

Asked why he had taken so much trouble to study the problems of paraplegia, Brando explained, "I felt this was an important dramatic situation. None of it was easy. This was about a man made completely helpless, worse than a baby or an animal. It's impossible to realize such terrible frustration and hopelessness unless you live like that." Despite his dedication Kramer and Zinnemann were at first worried about Brando's performances in the rehearsals because he mumbled his lines and gave little response to his fellow actors. But with the actual filming of his first scene he reduced co-star Teresa Wright to tears and won a minute of applause from the cast and crew. With no prior film experience Brando had been employing the stage technique of holding back in rehearsals and saving the projection for the performance. Brando was able to immediately prove himself not only a capable film actor but an exceptional one, completely oblivious to the camera and possessing that peculiar aura rare among actors in any media—that of drawing and holding attention merely by presence.

The Men has a direct and simply storyline. Brando appears early in the film as a young infantry lieutenant leading his platoon through an embattled European town. Considering the immediate area clear of the enemy the lieutenant advances into an open square. Within seconds a shot rings out—a sniper's bullet hits him in the lower back and in a fraction of a second the robust young man is reduced to being a paraplegic for the remainder of his life. In the hospital he is a sullen and resentful patient and in feel-

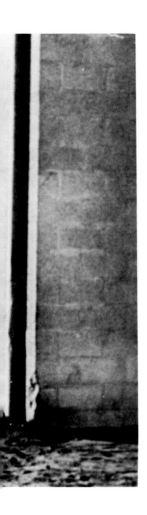

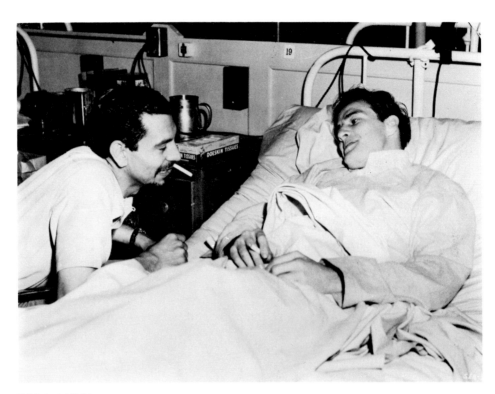

With Jack Webb

With Richard Erdman and Ray Teal

With Teresa Wright

With Teresa Wright

30

With Teresa Wright and Everett Sloane

ing sorry for himself he finds no sympathy from his fellow paraplegics. The film is semi-documentary in style and matter-of-fact in dealing with its central character. The lieutenant's pride and sensitivity makes difficult the task of readjustment. His reluctance to respond to treatment begins to diminish through the persistence of his fiancée (Teresa Wright), who refuses to give him up despite his wish that she do so. With her love and determination he begins to tackle the program of adjustment, exercising to build up the upper part of his body, learning to substitute a wheelchair for his lower limbs and to drive a specially equipped car. He decides to go through with the wedding, determined to take the vows standing up at the altar. But the wedding night is painfully disappointing and he returns to the hospital. Later he is involved in a drunk driving accident and disciplined by his fellow patients. Eventually he comes to realize that he has responsibilities, especially to

a wife who is also faced with the problems of being married to a paraplegic, a course she has accepted with full knowledge and considerable courage.

The film gets its effectiveness from the realism of its settings, its no-nonsense approach to its material and the superb performances of its players. Many people assumed Brando was actually a paraplegic acting out his own story rather than a professional actor, so convincing and non-theatrical was his essaying of the stricken young lieutenant. Teresa Wright was poignant as a bride who loved her man too much to be discouraged by her own doubts and fears, and Everett Stone was perfect as a doctor who knows he cannot show his sympathy. Also outstanding were Jack Webb, in one of his first film appearances, as a bitter and caustic paraplegic and Richard Erdman as a happy-go-lucky one, who smokes cigars, bets on horse races and figures he has "Never had it so good." *The Men* suc-

With Teresa Wright

ceeds in not being maudlin and also managing to be humorous and optimistic. It is a credit to Kramer, Foreman, Zinnemann and Brando, all of whom must have been aware that a film on such a topic had no chance of being a top box office attraction.

Brando managed to wring some humor out of his experiences at the hospital. He amused the men in the 32-bed ward in which he stayed by attempting to perform as a paraplegic on their terms, even going out with them in the evening

To the right of Brando: Jack Webb and Richard Erdman

With Teresa Wright

in a wheelchair. On one occasion he was with them in a local bar when a slightly inebriated, somewhat evangelistic woman cornered them with a long diatribe of sympathy. She labored them with the power of prayer and the value of hope and faith. Brando wheeled his chair closer to her, listening with rapture to her encouragement. Slowly and laboriously he lifted himself to his feet. He took a few slow, tortured steps and then burst into a vigorous tap dance. Those who were there claim the woman fainted.

A Charles K. Feldman Production, released by Warner Bros.
Produced by Charles K. Feldman.
Directed by Elia Kazan.
Screenplay by Tennessee Williams, adapted from Wil- Running time: 125 minutes.
liams' stage play by Oscar Saul.
Photographed by Harry Stradling.
Art direction by Richard Day.
Edited by David Weisbart.
Musical score by Alex North.

CAST:

Blanche DuBois	Vivien Leigh
Stanley Kowalski	Marlon Brando
Stella	Kim Hunter
Mitch	Karl Malden
Steve	Rudy Bond
Pablo	Nick Dennis
Eunice	Peg Hillias
A Collector	Wright King
A Doctor	Richard Garrick
The Matron	Anne Dere
Mexican Woman	Edna Thomas

Tennessee Williams, in the minds of most people the finest living American dramatist, has been well served by the film versions of his plays. In this respect he has been luckier than most playwrights and novelists, many of whom have reason to complain about the altering of their work when it is turned into movie material. The Williams plays have been almost literal in their transcription into film and the author himself has sometimes been involved in the writing of the screenplays. The first Williams play to be filmed was *The Glass Menagerie* in 1950, fol-

A STREETCAR NAMED DESIRE

(1951)

lowed by *A Streetcar Named Desire* (1951), *The Rose Tattoo* (1955), *Baby Doll* (1956), *Cat on a Hot Tin Roof* (1958), *Suddenly Last Summer* (1959), *The Fugitive Kind* (1960), *Summer and Smoke* (1961), *Sweet Bird of Youth* (1962), and *The Night of the Iguana* (1966). Williams also adapted his short story "The Milk Train Doesn't Stop Here Anymore" into a screenplay, *Boom*, filmed in 1968. Of all this material it might be argued that the most effective as a film is *A Streetcar Named Desire*.

Elia Kazan had directed the New York staging of the play but he did not want to be responsible for putting it on film. Kazan does not like to deal with the same subject twice but his friend Tennessee Williams, a very charming and persuasive man, finally convinced him he was the only man to make the picture. Kazan spent a few months working on a screen treatment that would open up the play but failed to arrive at a satisfactory means. He then decided that the best way to do it would be to take the original play and merely re-phrase it into the mechanics of a film shooting script. Scenarist Oscar Saul was hired to help Williams do this. The problem of casting was easily solved by Kazan using most of his original Broadway players. He rehired three of his principals—Marlon Brando, Karl Malden and Kim Hunter—and four of his supporting players—Rudy Bond, Nick Dennis, Peg Hillias and Edna Thomas. Jessica Tandy had played the leading role of Blanche DuBois in New York but Warner Brothers balked at the idea of Miss Tandy playing the part in the film. They were concerned about the box office potential of the vehicle—it did only mild business outside of the major cities—and they needed a star. The obvious solution was Vivien Leigh, who had been playing Blanche in the London staging of the play, with her then husband Sir Laurence Olivier

directing. The only problem now was that Miss Leigh arrived at the studio with her own interpretation of the part clearly set, and it was not what Kazan had in mind. Hers was a remote and fanciful concept whereas Kazan wanted a searingly realistic portrayal. The star and the director overcame their differences and the result was an Academy Award for Miss Leigh, her second. Somewhat ironically the elegant English actress won her first for playing another Southerner—Scarlett O'Hara in *Gone With the Wind*.

Tennessee Williams won the Pulitzer Prize and the New York Drama Critics award for *A Streetcar Named Desire* yet he says he considers the film a better interpretation of his material than the play. It might well be that the camera reveals more of the nuances of his subtle writing; certainly Blanche becomes even more pathetic when viewed closely and the brutal Stanley Kowalski more frightening. Much of the story concerns the effect these two characters have on each other, and Kazan's camera moves in and examines the anguish that could only be felt from a distance in the theatre.

The story begins with Blanche arriving in New Orleans and locating—after having taken a streetcar named Desire, transferring to one named Cemetery and getting off at Elysian Fields—the drab apartment of her sister Stella (Kim Hunter) in a murky section of the old French Quarter. The two sisters are different in every way—Blanche, much older, is a fragile neurotic given to affectations of morality and gentility, and Stella is a healthy, uncomplicated girl quite satisfied in her relationship with her crude Polish-American working-man husband Stanley. But he resents having a sister-in-law dumped on him and he quickly realizes Blanche is lying about her past life. Stanley is without sympathy and he ignores Stella's pleas that he be

35

With Vivien Leigh

With Vivien Leigh

With Kim Hunter and Vivien Leigh

With Kim Hunter

With Vivien Leigh

With Vivien Leigh

gentle with the self-deluding Blanche. She irritates him with her constant pretensions to an aristocratic background and when she tells of having to sell Belle Reve, the family estate, his only thought is for the money derived from the sale. He demands to see the papers and he tells Stella that under Louisiana's Napoleonic Code what belongs to one marriage partner belongs to the other: "It looks to me like you been swindled, baby, and when you get swindled under the Napoleonic Code I get swindled too. And I don't like to be swindled." Stanley then starts to rummage through Blanche's large traveling trunk and wonders how she, a small town school teacher, acquired so many dresses and fur pieces and jewelry.

Stanley forces information out of Blanche and finds that Belle Reve was lost on delinquent mortgages. Grandly she tells him: "There are thousands of papers stretching back over hundreds of years, affecting Belle Reve. As piece by piece our improvident grandfathers exchanged the land for their epic debauches. Till finally all that was left, was the house itself and about twenty acres of ground including a graveyard, to which now all but Stella and I have retreated." Further probing by Stanley reveals

cracks in her strange stories and he places inquiries in the town in which she lived. Meanwhile, life goes on in this awkward menage and Stanley makes no concessions to his guest. His poker playing friends come in for their weekly game and one of them, Mitch (Karl Malden) is smitten with Blanche. The roughneck batchelor is taken by her patrician airs and he tries to play the gentleman. As the poker game progresses Stanley gets drunk and truculent, hitting his wife, smashing their radio, and getting angry at Mitch for the attention he is paying Blanche. Stella and Blanche leave the apartment and go upstairs to stay with Stella's friend Eunice (Peg Hillias). Late at night, with the game over and the men gone, Stanley stands outside and yells for his wife. This—one of the most famous scenes in the film—amply demonstrates his magnetism: Stella appears at the top of the iron staircase in the front of the building and, despite his awful behavior, she slowly comes down. He falls to his feet and presses his face to her stomach, sobbing like a baby. He rises and she kisses him passionately as he cries, "Don't ever leave me, don't ever leave me, sweetheart, baby."

Stanley's investigations begin to bear fruit. He finds out sordid bits of information about

38

Blanche. It appears she was once married but that her husband, younger than she, died, and that she has had numerous affairs with men, many of them strangers passing through town. The evidence points to nymphomania and possibly prostitution, and being fired from her position as a school teacher for moral laxity. She seemingly has a weakness for very young men. All of this Stanley reveals to Mitch, which costs Blanche her one remaining chance of escape. It also costs Stanley his chance to get rid of Blanche, who has now been living with him and Stella for five months. When Stella leaves the apartment to go to the hospital to have a baby, the two foes are left to face each other. One evening, after much taunting, Stanley forces himself on Blanche and makes love to her. She tries to fight him off but he says, "We've had this date with each other from the beginning."

The final scenes of *A Streetcar Named Desire* show a doctor and a nurse arriving at the Kowalski apartment. They are from a mental institution and they have come for Blanche. She imagines they bring news from an old beau, someone who wants her and will rescue her, and she leaves the apartment on the arm of the doctor, timidly smiling at him and saying, "Whoever you are, I have always depended on the kindness of strangers." The tearful Stella angrily tells the unrepentant Stanley, "Don't you touch me. Don't you ever touch me again." Later, as she holds her baby in her arms she ignores Stanley as he calls for her. She goes to Eunice's apartment as she tells the baby, "We're not going back in there. Not this time. We're never going back. Never, never back, never back again." But as the voice of the brutish Stanley rings out, the audience can well assume that Stella will probably change her mind.

Despite its obvious stage origins, *A Streetcar*

With Vivien Leigh

With Kim Hunter

41

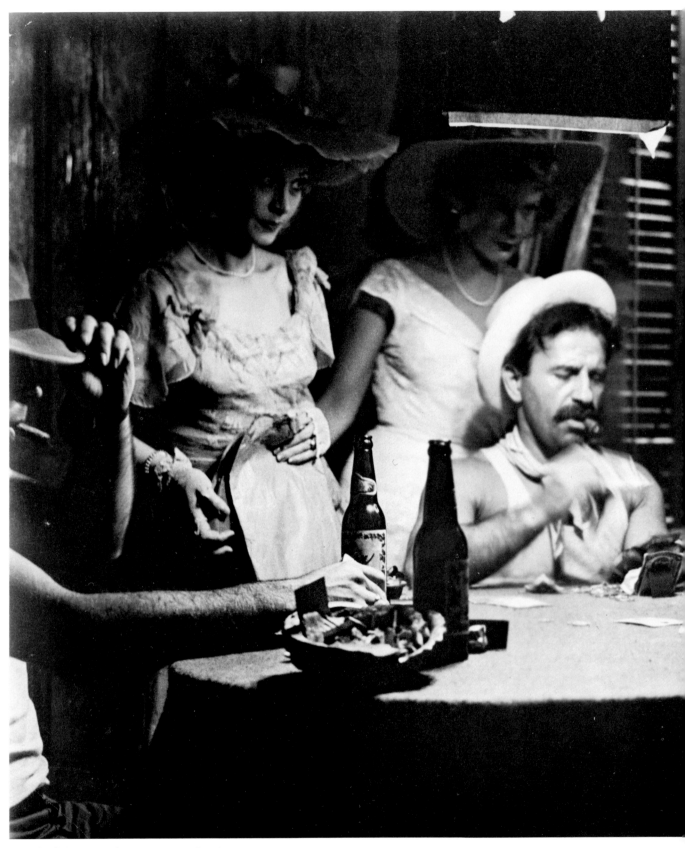

With Vivien Leigh, Kim Hunter and Nick Dennis

Named Desire is a film masterpiece. It is a credit to Elia Kazan that the long and difficult story, told largely in terms of dialogue, never falters in its tense pace. It is a cauldron of emotions, constantly sizzling. The technical credits are of the highest: the sets of Richard Day are a cunning combination of fantasy and realism and they allow veteran photographer Harry Stradling plenty of scope for haunting, artfully lit images. The film's musical score is particularly effective and the Capitol recording of its themes has since become one of the most sought-after collector's items. Alex North was new to Hollywood at this time although he had scored many stage plays and documentary films in New York, but his rich, jazz-tinted score for *Streetcar* quickly elevated him to the front rank of film composers.

On the acting level, *Streetcar* cannot be faulted, doubtless because all the players were long familiar with the material. Marlon Brando has often complained that the main problem with acting for the screen is that the actor is required to perform for the camera without being sufficiently comfortable with his part or his lines. When complimented about his performance in *Streetcar* he allows that if he was good as Kowalski it was because he thoroughly knew and understood the character and the meaning of every line. Brando has never been happy about being an actor, and much less than happy about the identification with Kowalski. He has, in fact, paid a price for the brilliance of that characterization and the image has haunted him. That people should consider him to be like that character appalls him. Says Brando, "Kowalski was always right, and never afraid. He never wondered, he never doubted himself. His ego was very secure. And he had the kind of brutal aggressiveness I hate. I'm afraid of it. I detest the character."

With Vivien Leigh, Kim Hunter, Peg Hillias and Karl Malden

With Karl Malden, Nick Dennis, Rudy Bond and Richard Garrick

A 20th Century–Fox Production.
Produced by Darryl F. Zanuck.
Directed by Elia Kazan.
Screenplay by John Steinbeck.
Photographed by Joe MacDonald.
Art direction by Lyle Wheeler and Leland Fuller.
Edited by Barbara McLean.
Musical score by Alex North.
Running time: 112 minutes.

CAST:

Emiliano Zapata	Marlon Brando
Josefa	Jean Peters
Eufemio Zapata	Anthony Quinn
Fernando	Joseph Wiseman
Don Nacio	Arnold Moss
Pancho Villa	Alan Reed
Soldadera	Margo
Madero	Harold Gordon
Pablo	Lou Gilbert
Señora Espejo	Mildred Dunnock
Huerta	Frank Silvera
Aunt	Nina Varela
Señor Espejo	Florenz Ames
Zapatista	Bernie Gozier
Col. Guajardo	Frank De Kova
General Fuentes	Joseph Granby
Innocente	Pedro Regas
Old General	Richard Garrick
Diaz	Fay Roope
Don Garcia	Harry Kingston
Officer	Ross Bagdasarian
Husband	Leonard George
Lazaro	Will Kuluva
Fuente's Wife	Fernanda Eliscu
Captain	Abner Biberman
C.O.	Phil Van Zandt
Garcia's Wife	Lisa Fusaro
Nacio's Wife	Belle Mitchell.

VIVA ZAPATA!

(1952)

Elia Kazan takes the credit for selling Darryl F. Zanuck on the idea of making *Viva Zapata!* With the success of *Gentleman's Agreement* and *Pinky* Kazan had proved that off-beat themes such as antisemitism and color bar were no longer taboo at the box office and he convinced Zanuck of the value of tackling political idealism with the story of the almost legendary Mexican revolutionary Emiliano Zapata. Once sold on the idea Zanuck plunged into the project with his characteristically aggressive and intense single-mindedness. He announced that he saw the story as a kind of spiritual adventure, one that should appeal to young boys as much as college professors. In this he was over-ambitious. Exciting and admirable though *Viva Zapata!* is, its motivations are likely to confuse children and appear simplistic to the educated. Zanuck was also unable to convince the Mexican government of his sincerity, particularly in dealing with historical material. The Mexicans have long objected to Hollywood depictions of their country and their people and the Zanuck film ended up being shot in Texas.

In fashioning his screenplay, John Steinbeck used as his guide Edgcomb Pinchon's book *Zapata the Unconquerable*, a fact that is not credited in the titles of the film. To give the film as true a feeling of authenticity as possible, Zanuck and Kazan studied the numerous photographs that were taken during the revolutionary years, the period between 1909 and 1919 when Zapata led his people in seeking restoration of land taken from them during the long dictatorship of President Porfirio Diaz. Kazan was especially impressed with the Casasola collection of photographs and he attempted to duplicate their visual style in his film. His setting of the meeting between Zapata and Pancho Villa and their staffs is almost an exact reproduction. *Viva Zapata!* was a departure in style from Kazan's previous films,

his first attempt at a large-scale, outdoors action picture and the results are greatly to his credit. He admits being influenced by Rosselini's *Paisan* but students might also sense some of the feeling of the films of Sergei Eisenstein. Kazan's film has a classicism about it, and he was greatly aided by the masterly photography of Joe Mac-Donald and a musical score by the esteemed Alex North, who as a young man had studied music in Mexico.

Marlon Brando read everything about Zapata that he could lay his hands on and he also spent time in the company of Mexicans in order to study their mannerisms and characteristics. He achieved a somewhat Indian appearance by slanting his eyelids and thickening his nose but his mastery of the role is much more mental than physical. His Zapata is a simple man, quiet and unemotional, who accepts the fact that fate has singled him out as a leader. The performance remains one of the most brilliant ever seen on the screen, with Brando subtly projecting the dedication and the anguish of the brooding Zapata.

The film begins with Zapata's first exposure to politics. He leads a delegation of peons from his village of Ayala to the ornate palace of President Diaz in Mexico City. There they make known their protests over the stealing of their lands by the wealthy, powerful landowners. Diaz addresses them paternally and advises them they must survey their boundaries before they bring legal action, something he knows they are incapable of doing. Zapata points this out to him, telling him they need his consent in order to cross fences. Diaz is rankled by the persistent Zapata and on the sheet of paper listing his visitors he ominously circles the name of this one man. Some time later Zapata and his brother Eufemio (Anthony Quinn) lead their villagers in a survey through their expropriated fields and as they do

With Joseph Wiseman and Lou Gilbert

so a squad of mounted police attack them, shooting and cutting down men, women and children indiscriminately. Zapata fights back, an act that immediately brands him an outlaw. He, his brother and some of their followers retreat to a mountain hideout. There they are located by a newspaperman named Fernando Aguirre (Joseph Wiseman), a political agitator who claims that his typewriter is the sword of the people. He brings news of Francisco Madero (Harold Gordon), exiled in Texas but sworn to lead a revolution to oust Diaz. Zapata then sends his friend Pablo (Lou Gilbert) to interview Madero and find out if he is worth following.

Stealing into Ayala at night, Zapata pays court to Josefa (Jean Peters), the daughter of a prominent citizen. She rebuffs him, even though she admits to being attracted to him, and tells him he must improve his social position before she might consider his proposal. Bent on reforming, Zapata goes to an influential friend, Don Nacio (Arnold Moss) and asks for his aid in dismissing the charges against him. This is arranged and Zapata goes to work for Don Nacio in his stables. Pablo returns from Texas and reports that Madero is sincere and wants Zapata as a leader in his revolution. Now intent on his courtship of Josefa, Zapata declines. He changes his mind later when he witnesses the whipping of children in the stables as punishment for minor misdeeds and the brutal killing of an old farmer by the police. When Senor Espejo (Florenz Ameo) refuses to consider him as a suitor to his daughter Zapata angrily leaves the village. He is immediately arrested by the police and led away with a rope around his neck. As the police walk him behind their horses through the countryside they are gradually joined by peons, who silently march along. The group swells into a

With Harry Kingston and Arnold Moss

mass and the police, realizing the situation, stop and remove the rope from Zapata's neck. Zapata also comes to a realization, that the people have chosen him as their leader and that he has no course but to accept. Destiny has singled him out.

Revolution overtakes Mexico. Police and soldiers are ambushed, armories are seized, ammunition trains are wrecked and looted and Zapata proves himself an able military tactician and an inspiring leader. After one particular battle a young boy is brought to Zapata and cited for his bravery in attacking a machine gun and saving the lives of his fellow soldiers. Zapata tells the boy he can have any prize he wants as a reward. The boy chooses the thing Zapata most prizes, his magnificent white horse, but true to his word Zapata lets the boy have him. Senor Espejo now approaches Zapata in the company of several officers of the revolution and tells him he has been instructed to offer him the rank of general. In accepting, Zapata also makes it impossible for Senor Espejo to reject him as a son-in-law. He and Josefa are married and on their wedding night he confesses to her that he is illiterate and that she must be his tutor as well as his wife.

Diaz flees Mexico and Madero is pronounced president. Zapata urges the new leader to give

50

back to the peons the lands they had lost under the previous regime but he finds Madero hesitant about this. The president tells him it will take time to legally return the lands and he tries to placate Zapata with the offer of an estate. It soon becomes apparent that Madero is a pawn in the hands of venal advisors, among them General Huerta (Frank Silvera). The president is unable to halt the growing power of his military aides, who seize the leadership of Mexico after they assassinate him. Again Zapata rises to lead his people. He joins forces with the celebrated Pancho Villa, the leader of the revolution in the northern provinces of Mexico. Villa has been pressed to take the presidency of Mexico but he declares his lack of interest in the office and suggests that Zapata become the president. Zapata finds the job of president onerous, especially when he has to listen to delegates complaining about the theft of their land. One of the people cited as a land grabber is his brother. Zapata elects to desert his office and return home but Fernando warns him, "If you leave today, your enemies will be here tomorrow." Zapata ignores the advice. In Ayala he reprimands his brother, now a drunken, swaggering bully who soon dies in a fight over a woman. Zapata senses the collapse of his life. In Mexico City, Fernando switches his allegiance to the military and urges them to get rid of Zapata. He draws up a plan and explains how this can be done.

With Margo, Lou Gilbert and Anthony Quinn

With Jean Peters

51

With Anthony Quinn, Lou Gilbert
and Harold Gordon

With Joseph Wiseman, Harold Gordon, Lou Gilbert and Margo

With Anthony Quinn

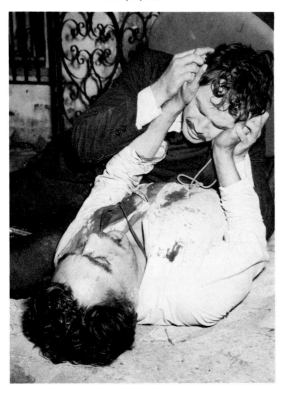

With Joseph Wiseman

Zapata is awakened one night and told that a colonel named Guajardo (Frank De Kova) wants to make a deal to desert to him and turn over his men and supplies. Zapata suspects a trap but he badly needs guns and ammunition. At a semi-ruined hacienda in Chinemeca the two men meet. Guajardo tells Zapta he has a gift for him—the white horse he gave to a boy as a prize for bravery. The horse appears and whinnies his recognition of his former master. Zapata buries his face in the horse's mane. Suddenly the horse rears and snorts. Zapata looks up and finds himself alone in the courtyard. Soldiers with rifles appear at every wall and a fusillade descends from every direction. Zapata is riddled with dozens of bullets. Fernando appears and orders the horse captured. But the horse, according to legend, was never captured and was sometimes seen in the mountains, helping the peons to believe that the spirit of Zapata was still alive.

Viva Zapata! is a greatly entertaining film, excitingly directed by Kazan who made its action sequences startlingly real and who allowed his actors full scope in developing their characters. Anthony Quinn won an Oscar as best supporting actor for his role as Eufemio Zapata, and Joseph Wiseman was magnificent as the sly, opportunistic Fernando. That Zanuck could not get permission to film in Mexico proved of no consequence. Kazan scouted the Texas border country and came across an area near the confluence of the Rio Grande and Pecos rivers that virtually duplicated the Mexican settings of the story. His art directors, with Mexican advisors, remodeled sections of the small Texas towns and they employed a large number of local people, many of whom were Mexican by blood, as extras.

Criticism has been levelled at *Viva Zapata!* on political grounds that it is a platforming of American liberal views. This may or may not be true, but certainly it is an idealized concept of Emiliano Zapata, whom historians claim was far more self-seeking and bloodier than as depicted by Zanuck, Steinbeck and Kazan. The Brando Zapata is a symbolic figure, a kind of Everyman of Mexican revolution, a titan arising from the ranks of the masses at the command of fate. Accepted in that spirit it is a poetic, powerful and truly moving picture.

The death of Zapata

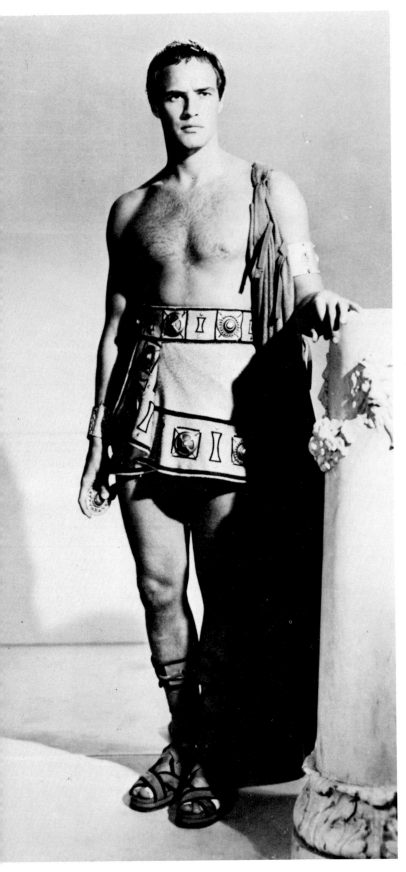

A John Houseman Production, released by MGM.
Produced by John Houseman.
Directed by Joseph L. Mankiewicz.
Written by William Shakespeare, adapted by Mankiewicz.
Photographed by Joseph Ruttenberg.
Art direction by Cedric Gibbons and Edward Carfagno.
Edited by John Dunning.
Musical score by Miklos Rozsa.
Running time: 123 minutes.

CAST:

Mark Antony	Marlon Brando
Brutus	James Mason
Cassius	John Gielgud
Julius Caesar	Louis Calhern
Casca	Edmond O'Brien
Calpurnia	Greer Garson
Portia	Deborah Kerr
Marullus	George Macready
Flavius	Michael Pate
Soothsayer	Richard Hale
Cicero	Alan Napier
Decius Brutus	John Hoyt
Metellus Cimber	Tom Powers
Cinna	William Cottrell
Trebonius	Jack Raine
Ligarius	Ian Wolfe
Artemiderus	Morgan Farley
Antony's Servant	Bill Phipps
Octavius Caesar	Douglas Watson
Lepidus	Douglas Dumbrille
Lucilius	Rhys Williams
Pindarus	Michael Ansara
Messala	Dayton Lummis
Strato	Edmund Purdom
First Citizen	Paul Guilfoyle
Second Ctizien	John Doucette
Third Citizen	Lawrence Dobkin
Fourth Citizen	Jo Gilbert

JULIUS CAESAR

(1953)

Of all the Shakespearean plays "Julius Caesar" is the one which most easily lends itself to film treatment. Its plotline is relatively simple and it is free of the digressions and sub-plots that cloud some of the Bard's other creations. It might also be argued that it is better suited to the screen than the stage, where its effectiveness has always rested on the delivery of its eloquent, passionate speeches. Only an intelligent filming can bring its processions and its street mobs and battle scenes up to the level of its oratory. Such a filming is the 1953 MGM version directed by Joseph L. Mankiewicz and produced by the esteemed John Houseman, himself a writer-director with experience in staging Shakespearean plays, including the famous modern-dress version of "Julius Caesar" at the Mercury Theatre. MGM quibbled with Mankiewicz and Houseman on only one point—the casting of Marlon Brando as Mark Antony. The studio, like so many people, was under the impression that the actor himself was somewhat like Stanley Kowalski, powerful but muddy of diction. To prove that such was not the case Mankiewicz had Brando record Antony's main speeches, which he then played to Dore Schary, then head of production at the studio, and a group of other chieftains. The point was easily won.

In preparing the screenplay Mankiewicz and Houseman decided that the film should be a literal treatment, with no interpolations for the sake of spectacle and no attempts at interpretation other than the author's. No lines were added to the original but a certain amount of editing was considered necessary, which has been the case ever since the play was first staged at the Globe Theatre in London almost four hundred years ago. It is, however, one of the shorter of Shakespeare's plays and the degree of trimming is usually minimal. Puns and repetitions accounted for most of the excisions; Shakespeare enjoyed provoking his Elizabethan audiences with puns, and his repetitions were deliberate because his audiences were often noisy, eating and drinking and milling around the theatre, and important points had to be constantly rephrased by the actors. Such restatements are superfluous in the modern theatre and even more so on film, where the close-up technique frequently obviates dialogue. Mankiewicz's deepest cuts were made in the play's fourth act, which brings the story to a climax with the Battle of Philippi. The verbiage spouted by messengers to relay news on the course of the battle was completely dropped in favor of actually showing the battle. This would doubtless have pleased Shakespeare, whose scripts contain very few stage directions.

Julius Caesar is set in Rome in 44 B.C. The city is rich with the spoils of its empire but it is also smoldering with political dissension, much of it brought on by Caesar (Louis Calhern) appointing himself dictator. Loyal to Caesar is Mark Antony (Brando) but Brutus (James Mason), an old friend of Caesar's, is torn between his personal feelings and his apprehension over Caesar's curtailing of democracy. The story begins on a festival day as Caesar and his entourage make their way to the stadium. On the way a soothsayer warns Caesar of "The Ides of March" but he is ignored. In the stadium Cassius (John Gielgud), the chief conspirator in a plot to overthrow the dictator, engages Brutus in conversation and implores him to join his cause. Brutus gradually becomes convinced as evidence is brought to his attention, and with the greatly respected Brutus on their side the conspirators feel confident in planning an assassination, on the ides of March (the middle of the month). On the previous day the city is swept by violent winds and rains.

Brutus agrees to the plot but vetoes Cassius' proposal that Mark Antony also die. After the conspirators have left, Brutus' wife Portia (Deborah Kerr) asks to know what it is that troubles him.

55

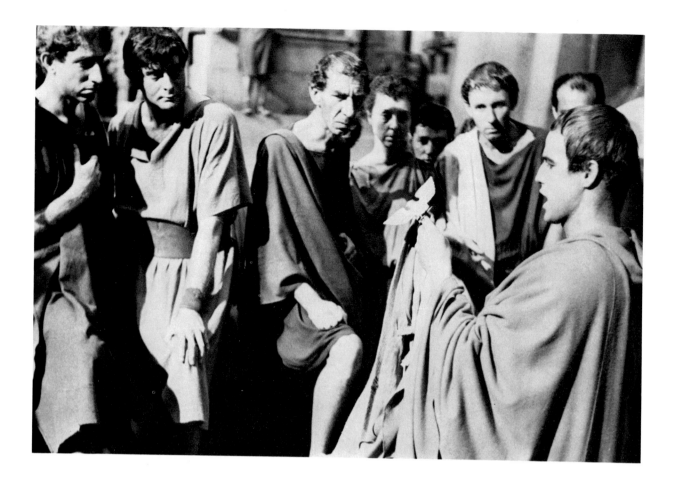

Caesar's wife, Calpurnia (Greer Garson), is also beset with premonitions of disaster and she begs him not to go to the Senate. But Caesar, his vanity being the fatal flaw in his character, believes his friends have gathered to offer him the crown of emperor and he proceeds. He again ignores the advice of the soothsayer and he leaves unopened a letter from a friend which lists the conspirators. Mark Antony is drawn away from the Senate on a pre-arranged plan, and the conspirators knife Caesar to death, the last thrust coming from Brutus. Later, Antony pretends a collaboration with the assassins and receives permission to speak at Caesar's funeral. Brutus addresses the Roman crowd and they accept his explanation that Caesar's death was necessary in order to curb his ambitions. Then Mark Antony mounts the platform and after several allusions to Brutus as "an honourable man" he shrewdly and passionately incites the citizens into a vow of vengeance.

The conspirators leave Rome, and Antony, with Octavius Caesar (Douglas Watson), seizes control of the city and purges it of suspected political enemies. Civil war breaks out, and in their camp at Macedonia Brutus and Cassius quarrel over their personal differences, particularly over Cassius' financial greed. The two men are somewhat reconciled by the news that Portia has committed suicide—she was Cassius' sister as well as Brutus' wife. Cassius yields to Brutus on a vital military point and they agree to meet the enemy on the plains of Philippi. On the night before the battle Brutus is visited by the ghost of Caesar and warned that they will meet at Philippi. The troops under the command of Cassius are defeated by those commanded by Mark Antony, and Cassius kills himself with the same dagger he used against Caesar. In the second stage of the battle Brutus and his men are defeated by the army of Octavius, and Brutus asks to be killed. They refuse and Brutus then places his sword in the hands of his servant and drives himself upon it. Later, as Antony comes to the tent

With William Cottrell, Edmond O'Brien, Jack Raines, Tom Powers, John Hoyt, John Gielgud and James Mason

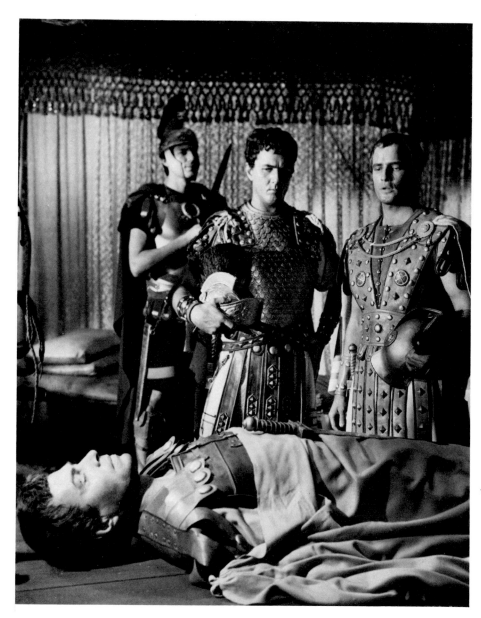

With James Mason and Douglas Watson

containing the body of his friend, he looks at Brutus and speaks the great tribute:

> This was the noblest Roman of them all:
> All the conspirators, save only he,
> Did that they did in envy of great Caesar;
> He only, in a general honest thought
> And common good to all, made one of them.
> His life was gentle, and the elements
> So mix'd in him that Nature might stand up
> And say to all the world, 'This was a Man!'

Shakespeare's "Julius Caesar" is a timeless play because its subject matter—political ambition and the manipulating of laws for personal gain—never dates. He clearly realized this with the lines:

> How many ages hence
> Shall this our lofty scene be acted o'er
> In states unborn and accents yet unknown.

Contemporary audiences sadly find nothing obscure about a dictator and his assassins and the abuse of government, or Shakespeare's obser-

With director Joseph L. Mankiewicz

vation, "The abuse of greatness is when it disjoins remorse from power." Any sincere, capable staging of *Julius Caesar* is bound to touch an intelligent audience, and this particular filming is a work of very high calibre. It is strikingly direct and unmarred by any artistic trickery. Its sets by Cedric Gibbon and Edward Carfagno, the musical score of Miklos Rozsa and the photography of Joseph Ruttenberg all represent MGM at that now sadly declined studio's professional apex. Any doubts about Marlon Brando being able to handle classical material were soon dispelled by his sharp, dark, compelling performance of Mark Antony. The passages in which he might have faltered, the long orations, proved to be those in which he was most inventive and persuasive. For those who thought *Julius Caesar* might be a hurdle in the path of Brando it became instead another stepping stone.

62

With Louis Calhern and, to the right of Brando, Alan Napier, Greer Garson, John Hoyt and Deborah Kerr.

A Stanley Kramer Company Production, released by Columbia Pictures Corporation.
Produced by Stanley Kramer.
Directed by Laslo Benedek.
Screenplay by John Paxton, based on a story by Frank Rooney.
Photographed by Hal Mohr.
Art direction by Walter Holscher.
Edited by Al Clark.
Musical score by Leith Stevens.
Running time: 79 minutes.

CAST:

Johnny	Marlon Brando
Kathie	Mary Murphy
Harry Bleeker	Robert Keith
Chino	Lee Marvin
Sheriff Singer	Jay C. Flippen
Mildred	Peggy Maley
Charlie Thomas	Hugh Sanders
Frank Bleeker	Ray Teal
Bill Hannegan	John Brown
Art Kleiner	Will Wright
Ben	Robert Osterloh
Wilson	Robert Bice
Jimmy	William Vedder
Britches	Yvonne Doughty
Gringo	Keith Clarke
Mouse	Gil Stratton, Jr.
Dinky	Darren Dublin
Red	Johnny Taragelo
Dextro	Jerry Paris
Crazy	Gene Peterson
Pidgeon	Alvy Moore
GoGo	Harry Landers
Boxer	Jim Connell
Stinger	Don Anderson
Betty	Angela Stevens
Simmonds	Bruno VeSoto
Sawyer	Pat O'Malley

THE WILD ONE

(1953)

The Wild One is considered to be the original motorcycle picture and years ahead of its time. Brilliantly staged and acted it was greeted with alarm by many film reviewers and social watchdogs who saw in it a hideous portent of things to come. The spate of motorcycle films didn't hit the screen until a dozen years later but *The Wild One* set the frightening style of the genre—the terrorizing of small communities by wolf packs of hoodlums on cycles. In making the picture Stanley Kramer was continuing his self-styled crusade in tackling America's sociological problems, and in selecting Marlon Brando to play the leading thug he did something that was both a blessing and a curse for the actor. Brando's black leather-jacketed Johnny, truculent, inarticulate and wooden-faced is now part of movie mythology. The image is ugly but distinct, and coming not long after the impact of *Streetcar* it somehow persuaded the public that the actor himself was something of a brute. Brando is far from pleased with this concept: "Before people meet me they feel they know me. I'm the kid who rides a motorcycle and wears a black leather jacket with crossbones painted on the back. I'm rude and unfeeling. When I'm an old man they'll still be asking me where my hot rod is."

The story line of *The Wild One* is simple; it begins with the arrival of a swarm of motorcyclists in a little town and it ends with their departure, but in the swift 79 minutes running time of the film the screen sizzles with their shocking behavior. The Black Rebels Motorcycle Club, a group of about forty members, comes to a noisy halt in front of Bleeker's Cafe. The cyclists have just been ordered away from a legitimate motorcycle meet in nearby Wrightsville and they are spoiling for trouble. A group of them race up and down the main street and force a car driven by an old man (Will Wright) off the street and into a pole, partially wrecking his car. The town policeman, Harry Bleeker (Robert Keith), also the owner of the cafe, tries to control the gang but he is intimidated by their leader, Johnny (Brando). Bleeker is not a courageous man and the cyclists rightly assume he is no match for them. They proceed to vandalize the town, riding their cycles in and out of stores, insulting the citizens and making raucous overtures to the girls, some of whom don't seem to mind the rough attention. Johnny follows a girl into Bleeker's Cafe and learns that she is the daughter, Kathie (Mary Murphy), of the owner-policeman. This cools him for the moment because he hates policemen but he is intrigued by the girl and he comes back later to make her a present of a stolen trophy. She refuses and he leaves, after which he ties the trophy on the back of his cycle.

Into this situation now comes Chino (Lee Marvin) and his group of cyclists, formerly a part of Johnny's gang but now a rival club. Chino and Johnny engage in an argument over the trophy and this leads to a savage brawl between the two in the street. Townspeople gather around to watch and one of them, Charlie Thomas (Hugh Sanders), gets his car overturned when he tries to drive through the mob. A group of citizens now demand that Bleeker do something to stop the hoodlums and he summons up enough courage to arrest Chino, who submits knowing his gang will get him out of jail. One of the girls in Chino's gang, Britches (Yvonne Doughty) attempts to win Johnny's attention but he is smitten with Kathie. She gradually yields to him, partly because she hates the town and wants to get out of it.

With the coming of the night hoodlums go on a rampage, smashing up saloons and stores and ripping out the phones in the police station, thereby stopping Bleeker from getting through to Wrightsville and help from the county sheriff. Johnny rescues Kathie from the molestations of

With Lee Marvin and Robert Keith

66

Chino's men and he takes her to a park. They talk for a while but his strange, inarticulate, angry manner scares her and she runs away from him. He runs after her and she slaps him when he catches her, then she runs off again, crying. Several townspeople see this and assume Johnny has attacked the girl. As he rides back into the town by himself a group of citizens attack him, drag him from his cycle and put him in a car. Kathie sees this and runs to get her father. Meanwhile the citizens take Johnny behind a store and beat him. Bleeker arrives with gun in hand and orders them to stop.

In trying to leave the town Johnny runs into a trap set by the citizens. Someone throws a tire iron at him and Johnny loses control of his cycle. It spins off the road and kills an old man. The crowd, now enraged, seizes Johnny and its mood suggests a lynching. He is saved from this by the arrival of Sheriff Singer (Jay C. Flippen), a man of calm authority who takes over the situation and quiets the town. Kathie speaks up for Johnny and explains that she was not attacked by him. Another citizen confesses that he saw someone throw the tire iron and that the acci-

With Yvonne Doughty

With Yvonne Doughty

To the left, Hugh Sanders, and to the right, Lee Marvin. The tall cyclist is Jerry Paris, now a director

Central is Jay C. Flippen. To his right—Hugh Sanders and Robert Keith

dent was not Johnny's fault. Singer frees Johnny but the badly shaken cyclist is unable to put into words any gratitude he might feel.

Sheriff Singer dismisses the hoodlums and warns them never to return to the county. He is an effective policeman but there is nothing in his manner to suggest that he understands the motorcyclists or the causes of their behavior. Johnny attempts to say goodbye to Kathie and to thank her father for coming to his rescue. But again he is choked by his lack of ability to communicate, to show any feeling other than a tough bravado. As he drives out of the town his mood is sullen—and to the audience he is an enigma.

Is he at all repentant? Will his future be affected by his experiences of the previous two days?

The Wild One hit America with a wallop. Exhibitors were afraid to show the picture lest it appeal only to the kind of customers who were the subject of the film, the kind who vandalized their theatres. The film actually did good business, mostly as an item of somewhat horrific fascination. In England, *The Wild One* was banned by the British Board of Film Censors, who felt that it was an all too graphic exercise in how to bottle up and terrorize a small town and that it might incite youngsters to riot. The British ban was not lifted until fourteen years later.

The sad onlooker is Will Wright

An excellent piece of film making, *the Wild One* is the high point in the career of its director, Laslo Benedek, a Hungarian, writer-photographer who directed his first Hollywood picture in 1948. Benedek's record as a director is meagre and undistinguished except for this one film. In getting this particular story into focus Benedek was able to do some direct research. The film is based on an actual incident, the raiding and vandalizing of the town of Hollister, California, in the summer of 1947 by a gang called the Anglenos, possibly the forerunners of the Hell's Angels. Scenarist John Paxton went to Hollister to talk to the townspeople and after he had written his script he went there again in the company of Benedek. The result

of all the research was a film with little narrative or continuity but almost totally impressionistic. It was a departure in style in American film making and it disturbed audiences of 1953 because of the lack of punishment or reformation of the vicious vandals. It was a sign that *things* were changing, both on the screen and in American life. Says Benedek, "The subject isn't juvenile delinquency, it's youth without ideals, without goals, which doesn't know what to do with the enormous energy which it possesses. What I tried to do in my picture was show that if you react with similar violence, you lose. That the vigilante attitude is useless, you just end up with an even greater problem. The film is not only about the cyclists,

70

it's about townspeople, merchants and policemen who behave badly and it's about the dangers of the white backlash mentality."

The Wild One draws a lot of its effectiveness from Marlon Brando's portrait of the tough, crude, inexpressive, hopeless Johnny, a characterization that met with much response among contemporary youngsters. But Brando himself is not an admirer of the picture: "I think it was a failure. We started out to do something very worthwhile, to explain the psychology of the hipster. But somewhere along the way we went off the track. The result was that instead of finding why young people tend to bunch into groups that seek expression in violence, all that we did was show the violence."

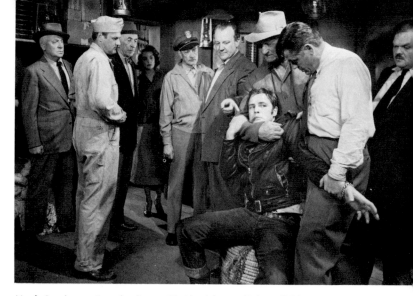

Hugh Sanders points the finger. To his right are Robert Keith, Mary Murphy and Will Wright

With Jay C. Flippen, Robert Keith, Mary Murphy

With Mary Murphy

A Sam Spiegel Production, released by Columbia Pictures.
Produced by Sam Spiegel.
Directed by Elia Kazan.
Screenplay by Budd Schulberg, based on articles by Malcolm Johnson.
Photographed by Boris Kaufmann.
Art direction by Richard Day.
Edited by Gene Milford.
Musical score by Leonard Bernstein.
Running time: 108 minutes.

CAST:

Terry Malloy	Marlon Brando
Father Barry	Karl Malden
Johnny Friendly	Lee J. Cobb
Charley Malloy	Rod Steiger
Kayo Dugan	Pat Henning
Edie Doyle	Eva Marie Saint
Glover	Leif Erickson
Big Mac	James Westerfield
Truck	Tony Galento
Tillio	Tami Mauriello
Pop Doyle	John Hamilton
Mott	Heldabrand
Moose	Rudy Bond
Luke	Don Blackman
Jimmy	Arthur Keegan
Barney	Abe Simon
J.P.	Barry Macollum
Specs	Mike O'Dowd
Gilette	Marty Balsam
Slim	Fred Gwynne
Tommy	Thomas Handley
Mrs. Collins	Anne Hegira

Prior to *On the Waterfront* American film makers had largely avoided the fields of industry, trade unionism and labor organization. These

ON THE WATERFRONT

(1954)

were considered dangerous fields to tread and not a likely source of entertainment. *On the Waterfront* was the first film to tackle these themes and it took courage on the part of producer Sam Spiegel, director Elia Kazan, and writer Budd Schulberg to venture into what was, and still is, an explosive area. Their film has sometimes been attacked as being anti-unionism and pro-fascist. It is nothing of the kind. *On the Waterfront* is a straightforward indictment of labor racketeering, of individuals who manipulate for their own gain the masses of under-educated, inarticulate laborers, in this instance the dock workers of New York. If anything, it urges the working man to fight for his rights and control his own destiny, rather than be a pawn in the ruthless system of bribes and kick-backs and exorbitant loans.

Budd Schulberg prepared the screenplay from his own story, which in turn was based upon a series of newspaper articles by Malcolm Johnson for the New York *Sun*. Mr. Johnson won a Pulitzer Prize in 1949 for this exposé of dockland corruption and labor conditions, and he also worked as an advisor in the making of the film. More than anyone else the credit for bringing *On the Waterfront* into being belongs to Elia Kazan. He had had the idea of doing a film about New York longshoremen while working with playwright Arthur Miller—Kazan directed "All My Sons," and "Death of a Salesman"—and Miller eventually came up with a story called "The Hook." This would have been the basis for their dockland picture except that the two men came to a parting of the ways in 1952 when Kazan gave testimony to the Un-American Activities Committee about Communist infiltration in American show business. This did not sit well with Miller. However, the playwright later uti-

lized his own findings on waterfront characters in his "A View from the Bridge." Kazan picked up the cudgel when he read Schulberg's story and the two agreed to collaborate. They made forays into the area of the story, the docks of New York and of Hoboken, New Jersey, and interviewed workers and unionists. After Schulberg had completed his script Kazan made the decision to film it in these same, actual settings. The film company was closely watched all through the filming and Kazan recalls that it was an uneasy and sometimes violent atmosphere. The longshoremen watched as their lives were being filmed and Kazan admits he had to engage in a certain amount of corruption himself, paying off a few individuals.

On the Waterfront is basically the story of one man, Terry Malloy, a young dock worker with a little, and unsuccessful, experience as a boxer but not much intelligence or purpose. He loafs around the docks on his own time, vaguely discontented about his life and revealing a tender streak in his otherwise tough manner as he tends his collection of pigeons caged on the roof of his tenement building. His brother Charley (Rod Steiger), a slick opportunistic lawyer, works for the local dockers' union, headed by Johnny Friendly (Lee J. Cobb), a breezily arrogant racketeer. Friendly takes an affectionate interest in Terry and tries to make things easy for him. He also takes advantage of Terry by involving him in the killing of an uncooperative docker. Terry unwittingly sets the trap for the man, who is then hurled from a rooftop because he allowed himself to be interviewed by a crime investigating commission.

Terry's alienation from the crooked union leaders starts when he meets the dead man's sister, Edie (Eva Marie Saint), and realizes the

73

With John Hamilton and Pat Henning

With Lee J. Cobb

With Tommy Handley and Eva Marie Saint

With Tommy Handley

With Rod Steiger

With Karl Malden

With Pat Hingle and Eva Marie Saint

With Rod Steiger

grief he has brought into her life. She asks his help in bringing the racketeers to justice, as does Father Barry (Karl Malden), a tough-minded waterfront priest. When another longshoreman is murdered, by having a heavy packing case "accidentally" dropped on him in the hold of a freighter, Father Barry defies the abuse of union hirlings and gives the last rites at the scene of the crime. And it is Terry who comes to the aid of the priest and knocks down a docker trying to stop the service. The angry priest looks around at the silent, sullen workers on the ship and berates them, "Boys, this is my church. And if you don't think Christ is down here on the waterfront—in the shape-up—you don't know nothing!" This is a poweful scene and a magnificent statement of Christianity.

As Terry becomes increasingly critical of the vicious union, and more and more in love with Edie, his brother Charley is instructed to warn him and silence him. The two brothers sit in the back of a car and talk. Terry now sees things more clearly than before and he realizes the true character of Charley, and how his brother had betrayed him in his early boxing career, "It was you, Charley . . . I could have been a contender, I could have been somebody, instead of a bum—which is what I am." This, too, is another of On the Waterfront's great scenes and one by which Marlon Brando is well remembered, and most mimicked by the impersonators. Yet another stunning scene is the one where Terry admits to Edie his part in the killing of her brother, and as he talks to her his words are drowned by the loud roars of a ship's whistle. It is a marvelous device on the part of Kazan and it jarringly conveys the pain and the shock of Terry and Edie. With her understanding and her love, he finds a new lease on life, and when his brother is brutally murdered—left hanging by a meat hook on a wall—Terry decides to testify against the racketeers at a hearing before the Crime Commission.

Terry's testimony spells the end of Johnny Friendly and his hoodlums, although a brief scene in which an affluent gentleman watches the hearings on television in his plush home and switches off the set when Friendly makes a fool of himself on the witness stand, clearly implies that it is not the end of high-level racketeering on the docks. The next day Terry goes to his job and he is ostracized by his fellow workers. He then enters the office of the union leader and

With Eva Marie Saint

engages Friendly in a long, savage brawl. Terry wins the fight and although battered and bleeding, barely able to walk, he goes about his job and his fellow workers, now impressed by his courage, follow him back to work. The crooked union is, at least for the moment, broken.

On the Waterfront is one of the great American films, not merely because it courageously sheds a bold light on a vast injustice right on its very doorstep, but because it is a skillful piece of film drama. It is Kazan at the very peak of his career, at the time when he was most capable of getting vital, compelling performances from actors. This aspect of filming no longer seems to interest him to the same degree, but at the time of making this film Kazan was still active with the celebrated Actor's Studio in New York. He was one of its prime forces, and largely responsible for the Stanislavsky-inspired "Method." Brando was a product of that system and his performance in this film brought him an Oscar and universal praise. Says Kazan, "To my way of thinking, Brando's performance in *On the Waterfront* is the best male performance I've ever seen in my life." Kazan had given a verbal commitment to Frank Sinatra to play Terry Malloy, Sinatra having recently made a great impact with his dramatic performance in *From Here to Eternity,* but shortly before filming Kazan learned that Brando was available and he then broke his promise to Sinatra, to the loud protestations of the volatile singer. Brando claims that it wasn't until the first day of shooting that he consolidated his ideas on playing Malloy.

Elia Kazan wisely gave his film a documentary appearance. Such a story called for realism and Kazan had prior experience in filming on location with *Boomerang* (1947), made entirely in Stamford, Connecticut, and *Panic in the Streets* (1950), filmed for the most part in New Orleans. He hired the Polish-born, New York-based cinematographer Boris Kaufman and received from him photography of arresting starkness. Kazan also managed to persuade Leonard Bernstein to write the musical score, the only film so far to include the work of this esteemed musician. Bernstein's modernistic, symphonic score has received some criticism for occasionally overpowering the picture but for the most part it is a valuable, dramatic comment, later made into an orchestral suite and several times recorded.

But the real value of *On the Waterfront* is

With Lee J. Cobb

With Lee J. Cobb

With Karl Malden and Eva Marie Saint

80

Marlon Brando's performance, and what makes it vital and fascinating is his depiction of a moral awakening. His Terry Malloy is tough, occasionally stupidly stubborn, vulnerable, masking his sensitivity with arrogance and every now and then showing a flash of charm and humor. It is a cunningly controlled piece of acting; Malloy has never thought much about life but he is driven to a point where he must take stock, and he sees the light. This might be said to be a story of redemption, but in simpler terms it is the story of an ordinary man finding the courage to stand up and be counted. As portrayed by Brando he is touchingly believable.

With Eva Marie Saint

Brando striking the famous Napoleonic pose, something he did not do in the film

A 20th Century–Fox Production.
Produced by Julian Blaustein.
Directed by Henry Koster.
Screenplay by Daniel Taradash, based on the novel by Annemarie Selinko.
Photographed in CinemaScope and De Luxe Color by Milton Krasner.
Art direction by Lyle Wheeler and Leland Fuller.
Edited by William Reynolds.
Musical score by Alex North.
Running time: 110 minutes.

CAST:

Napoleon	Marlon Brando
Desirée	Jean Simmons
Josephine	Merle Oberon
Bernadotte	Michael Rennie
Joseph Bonaparte	Cameron Mitchell
Julie	Elizabeth Sellars
Paulette	Charlotte Austin
Mme. Bonaparte	Cathleen Nesbitt
Marie	Evelyn Varden
Mme. Clary	Isobel Elsom
Talleyrand	John Hoyt
Despreaux	Alan Napier
Oscar	Nicolas Koster
Etienne	Richard Deacon
Queen Hedwig	Edith Evanson
Mme. Tallien	Carolyn Jones
Fouche	Sam Gilman
Louis Bonaparte	Larry Craine
Caroline Bonaparte	Judy Lester
Lucien Bonaparte	Richard Van Cleemput
Elisa Bonaparte	Florence Dublin
Baron Morner	Louis Borell
Count Brahe	Peter Bourne
Queen Sofia	Dorothy Neumann
Barras	David Leonard
Princess Sofia	Siw Paulsson

DESIREE

(1954)

Caulaincourt	Lester Matthews
Von Essen	Gene Roth
General Becker	Colin Kenny
Jerome	Peter Raynolds
Pope Pius VII	Leonard George
Count Reynaud	Richard Garrick
Marie Louise	Violet Rensing
Montel	A. Cameron Grant

By 1954 Marlon Brando had become, whether he liked it or not, a *film star*, and in Hollywood's thinking he was now a property to be handled with commercial care. His first six films might all be described as off-beat or prestigious items but now it was time for Brando to appear in the kind of films in which a film star would star. *Desiree* is just such a vehicle, lavish and handsomely packaged. It is a story-book historical romance with Brando as Napoleon Bonaparte and Jean Simmons as the girl of the title who loves and, supposedly, inspires him. Brando was not greatly enthusiastic about playing the role but he had put himself in a position with 20th Century–Fox in which he could not refuse. The studio had signed him for *The Egyptian*, another costume picture with a huge budget, with Brando playing the lead. Brando backed out of the film just prior to the commencement of shooting, claiming reasons of health, forcing Fox to quickly get a replacement. They gambled on the relatively unknown Edmund Purdom and as Peter Ustinov puts it, "Charming though that was, it wasn't quite the same thing." *The Egyptian* was not a success and Purdom's Hollywood career was short lived. Brando had no moral choice but to accept Fox's request that he do *Desiree,* and it is fortunate for the studio that he did because this king-size soap opera has little value other than his performance.

The fanciful yarn begins in 1794. Desiree Clary, a lively, pretty girl of seventeen, runs through the streets of Marseilles and arrives home late for supper. She tells her mother (Isobel Elsom), her sister Julie (Elizabeth Sellars), and her stuffy brother Etienne (Richard Deacon) that she has been walking in the park with a Corsican named Joseph (Cameron Mitchell). The Clarys, an affluent family, are shocked by her behavior, more so when she tells them she has invited Joseph and his brother to visit them the next day. The brother is a young general called Napoleone Buonaparte, whose uniform is somewhat shabby but whose manner is strangely compelling. Napoleone sees that his brother and Julie are attracted to each other and he tells Desiree that he approves of such a union because of the wealth of the Clarys. Desiree is likewise smitten with Napoleone, a fact which she commits to her diary. The diary serves as a transition device throughout the film and succinctly tells much of the story.

A few days later, in the Clarys' silk store, Desiree shows Napoleone material suitable for her sister's wedding gown when soldiers enter and inform Napoleone that they have a warrant for his arrest, and that his friend Robespierre has been executed on the guillotine. He gives Desiree the address of his family and asks her to let them know what has happened. She visits the Buonapartes and meets his mother, three more brothers and three sisters. Only the mother (Cathleen Nesbitt) and Louis (Larry Crain) seem concerned about the news, and Louis seems relieved that now Napoleone won't be able to force him into the army.

Desiree is awakened one night by the sound of whistling beneath her window. It's Napoleone and she ecstatically rushes out to meet him. He tells her that he has been assigned to hunting

With Elizabeth Sellars, Cameron Mitchell and Jean Simmons.

With Jean Simmons

With Jean Simmons and Evelyn Varden

down royalists, which he disgustedly looks upon as police work and not fitting for an artillery expert. Desiree tells him that he might resign his commission and go to work for the Clarys in their store. This suggestion also meets with his disgust. Brother Etienne is disturbed by the talking and appears at an upper window. Napoleone asks for Desiree's hand in marriage but Etienne, the head of the household, refuses. Napoleone then tells her they will be married despite this refusal but first he must go to Paris and convince the war ministry to put him in charge of the Italian campaign; with that he departs.

Months go by and Desiree hears nothing from her beloved. Her family tease her, as she embroiders things for her trousseau, and she finally decides to go to Paris and locate Napoleone. She goes to La Chaumiere, where Mme. Tallien (Carolyn Jones) caters to the famous, because she has heard Napoleone—who has now shortened his name to Napoleon Bonapart—is often seen there. She is refused admittance by the doorman and while standing outside she watches Josephine Beauharnais (Merle Oberon) enter. Desiree finally gets in through the amused help of Gen-

With Richard Van Cleemput and Cathleen Nesbitt

With Jean Simmons

With Jean Simmons (behind central figure) and Merle Oberon

85

With Merle Oberon

With Jean Simmons

With Jean Simmons and Michael Rennie

eral Jean-Baptiste Bernadotte (Michael Rennie). When she overhears that Napoleon and Josephine are set to be married Desiree runs from La Chaumiere in tears. She is about to jump from a bridge into the Seine when Bernadotte, who has followed her, talks her out of suicide. Bernadotte asks to see her again but she rebuffs him and tells him she has had enough of generals.

The scene shifts to Rome where Desiree visits her sister Julie and her husband Joseph Bonapart, now the French ambassador to Italy. She writes in her diary that Napoleon appears to be conquering the world, and when she next meets him she rejects his suggestion that they resume their friendship, particularly in view of his apparent discontent with Josephine because she cannot bear him a child. Napoleon clearly envies the fact that his brother Joseph now has a son. Bernadotte is relentless in his courting of Desiree and she agrees to marry him. Bernadotte, now a Marshall of France, quarrels with Napoleon over his dictatorial ambitions and refuses to support him, but Napoleon wins him over with his talk of reforms and improvements for the French people.

Napoleon does not relax in his ambitions. Once elected First Consul of the Republic he consolidates his power and has himself crowned Emperor in a magnificent ceremony at Notre Dame. Shortly after becoming the Emperor he announces the dissolution of his marriage with the barren Josephine and his intention to marry Austrian Princess Marie-Louise von Hapsburg. Desiree befriends Josephine and once more rejects Napoleon's advances. In 1810 a Swedish delegation arrives at the Bernadotte home and informs the Marshall that their government has chosen him as heir to the throne of Sweden. Bernadotte accepts and the family move to Stockholm, to the annoyance of Napoleon, who is affronted by Bernadotte's surrender of his French citizenship.

Life in Stockholm does not please Desiree; she dislikes the coldness of the country and the formality of its people. After some months she returns to Paris and a reclusive life. On New Year's Eve (1811–1812) Desiree attends a party at which Napoleon displays his new son and announces his plans to invade Russia and eventually attack England. Bernadotte is partly responsible for Napoleon's defeat in Russia, having advised the Czar on tactics. On his return to Paris Napoleon asks Desiree to write a letter to Bernadotte and plead with him to join the French cause. Bernadotte takes the opposite view and Napoleon is again defeated, this time by allied European forces. Bernadotte comes to Paris, where he is reunited with his wife and where he is among those who sentence Napoleon to exile on Elba. Napoleon escapes from the island and raises a new army, still intent on his master plan for a United States of Europe. He approaches Paris with threats of destruction and makes his headquarters at Malmaison. It is there that Desiree goes to meet him and convince him that his surrender would be in the best interests of France. With this persuasion he hands over his sword.

Desiree is an enjoyable film if taken not too seriously. It might have been better had it not dealt with so well documented a giant of history as Napoleon. That a girl named Desiree was married to his brother is a fact, but that she was able to persuade the iron-willed dictator to give up his ambitions and accept exile is an absurd flight of fancy. The film is admirable on the technical level, with superb sets and costumes, but as drama it is too pedestrian and talkative. It derives much of its strength from the charming performance of a radiant Jean Simmons, who is on screen for most of the long story and believably develops from a naïve girl to a woman of assurance. From Marlon Brando, *Desiree* received an astonishing portrait of Napoleon. Critics have always been divided in their reaction, some feeling

With Evelyn Varden, Jean Simmons and Lester Matthews

that it was a masterfully controlled performance while others felt that Brando was toying with the role and merely enjoying himself. A major surprise for many people was his clarity of diction; gone was the thick-mouthed mumbler of *The Wild One*. Brando's Napoleon speaks with a soft and lyrical voice, crisply enunciating his words in a precise English accent. His model was obviously Claude Rains. Assuming a French accent would have made the characterization ludicrous, but Brando's use of a quiet, measured English accent somehow gave the role its chilly, man-of-destiny implication. Brando also wisely avoided the posturing that mars many depictions of Napoleon, at no time striking the celebrated hand-in-jacket pose. In this fictional framework Brando is able to suggest the cool, calculating, compulsive, lonely man Napoleon might well have been.

A Samuel Goldwyn Production, released by MGM.
Produced by Samuel Goldwyn.
Directed and written by Joseph L. Mankiewicz, based on the play with book by Jo Sterling and Abe Burrows, from a story by Damon Runyon.
Photographed in CinemaScope and Eastman Color by Harry Stradling.
Art direction by Joseph Wright.
Choreography by Michael Kidd.
Edited by Daniel Mandell.
Music supervised and conducted by Jay Blackton.
Music and lyrics by Frank Loesser.
Songs: Fugue for Tin Horns; Follow the Fold; The Oldest Established; I'll Know; Pet Me, Poppa; Guys and Dolls; Adelaide; If I Were a Bell; A Woman in Love; Take Back Your Mink; The Crap Game Dance; Luck Be a Lady; Sue Me; Sit Down, You're Rockin' the Boat.
Running time: 149 minutes.

CAST:

Sky Masterson	Marlon Brando
Sarah Brown	Jean Simmons
Nathan Detroit	Frank Sinatra
Adelaide	Vivian Blaine
Nicely-Nicely Johnson	Stubby Kaye
Benny Southstreet	Johnny Silver
Big Jule	B. S. Pully
Harry the Horse	Sheldon Leonard
Lt. Brannigan	Robert Keith
Arvide Abernathy	Regis Toomey
Lverne	Veda Ann Borg
General Cartwright	Kathryn Givney
Rusty Charlie	Dan Dayton
Angie the Ox	Joe McTurk
Society Max	George E. Stone
Calvin	Kay Kuter
Agatha	Mary Alan Hokanson
Louie	John Indrisano
Mission Member	Stapleton Kent
Pitch Man	Earle Hodgins
Waiter	Harry Tyler

GUYS AND DOLLS

(1955)

Immediately after the Broadway opening of "Guys and Dolls" in November of 1950, various Hollywood studios began bidding for the film rights, but the producers, Cy Feuer and Ernie Martin, were in no hurry to dispose of them. It was obvious that they were in possession of a smash musical that might run for years, and a filming might short-change its stage potential. Feuer and Martin could hardly have been more right. *Guys and Dolls* ran for a solid three years on Broadway, followed by a similar run in England and a North American tour which covered sixty cities. In the first five years of its life the musical grossed over sixteen million dollars.

Samuel Goldwyn had not been among the original bidders. He waited until the producers announced the possible closing date of the Broadway run and then made his move. Goldwyn had heard that another film producer had offered $800,000 but that the deal had not been negotiated. With that he instructed his representatives to hand Feuer and Martin a sealed bid of $1,000,000 cash against ten per cent of the world gross, and within minutes Goldwyn acquired the movie rights to *Guys and Dolls*. He allocated another $4,500,000 for the budget and raised Hollywood eyebrows by hiring a director who had never before handled a musical subject, Joseph L. Mankiewicz, and a pair of stars, Marlon Brando and Jean Simmons, with no song-and-dance experience. It was expected that Goldwyn would have the songs of Brando and Simmons dubbed by professional singers but he reasoned that since the songs were part of the narrative, revealing story and character points, it was more important that they use their own voices and their dramatic ability to interpret the songs.

Greatly successful though it had been on the stage *Guys and Dolls* was not a *natural* for screen treatment. The Damon Runyon yarns and their assortment of weirdly amusingly edge-of-the-underworld characters are very much New York oriented, aside from which there is a cynical, bitter flavor to the material—all highly suitable to the sophisticated stage but not to the commercial cinema. Goldwyn and Mankiewicz agreed the script needed revision and softening as a screenplay, making the flinty characters somewhat more appealing. Composer-lyricist Frank Loesser added three songs to his original score, "Pet Me, Poppa," "Adelaide," and "A Woman in Love," and of the original Broadway stars only Vivian Blaine was used in the film. Two of the original supporting players, Stubby Kaye as "Nicely-Nicely Johnson" and Johnny Silver as "Benny Southstreet" here made their film debuts. The important characterization of "Nathan Detroit," performed with great acclaim on Broadway by Sam Levene was handed to Frank Sinatra, an obvious commercial ploy but one which robbed the part of the sting of the original concept.

The Mankiewicz version holds firm to the plotline of the play as written by Jo Sterling and Abe Burrows. It opens with Sergeant Sarah Brown (Jean Simmons) exhorting a listless crowd on the street to enter her Save-a-Soul Mission, and failing to get a single convert. Nearby, Nicely-Nicely Johnson and Benny Southstreet meet Harry the Horse (Sheldon Leonard) who asks them if they know the whereabouts of Nathan Detroit's crap game because he's got five thousand dollars from collecting the reward on his father and wants to gamble. They tell him Lt. Brannigan (Robert Keith) is out to get Detroit but that the irrepressible Nathan will doubtless stage a game someplace soon. Nathan finds the only place he can get is a garage where the owner wants a thousand dollar advance in cash, which Nathan doesn't happen to have. He doesn't even have

With Jeam Simmons, Frank Sinatra and Vivian Blaine

enough money to buy an anniversary present for Adelaide (Vivian Blaine), the chorus girl to whom he's been engaged for fourteen years. An idea for raising a thousand dollars comes to him when he learns Sky Masterson (Brando) is in town. Masterson is a gambler with a reputation for taking on any bet. In a conversation with Nathan, Masterson makes the claim that all women are alike. Nathan challenges the point and he bets Masterson that he couldn't, for example, persuade a certain Salvation Army doll to go with him on his upcoming trip to Havana, Cuba.

Masterson visits the Save-a-Soul Mission. Sarah is about to admit defeat when Masterson promises to produce a dozen sinners for her meeting next Thursday if she'll have dinner with him on Wednesday evening. She accepts and then learns that the dinner is in Havana. After a lot of hedging she goes with him, and after a few drinks in a Havana nightclub Sarah undergoes a wild

change of character, dancing, turning amorous and even taking part in a brawl. They return to New York to find crapshooters gathering for the Big Game, and thinking that Masterson has had something to do with organizing it Sarah angrily takes her leave of him. But she is in love with him and relieved when told he is innocent, although still concerned about the fate of her mission hanging on the appearance of a dozen spiritual derelicts.

To make good his pledge, Masterson joins the crap game, now being staged underground in a city sewer. He gives Nathan the thousand dollars, which the broke-but-lucky chancer then turns into a bundle of winnings. He and Masterson and the crapshooters take their places in the pews of the mission and Sarah is able to keep her commission. Masterson decides not to stay, but when Sarah is told by Nathan that it was he who caused Masterson to take her to Havana on a bet

With Jean Simmons

With Regis Toomey, Jean Simmons, Johnny Silver and Stubby
Kaye

With Jean Simmons

With Jean Simmons

93

With Jean Simmons

With Jean Simmons

With Frank Sinatra

With Sheldon Leonard, Stubby Kaye, and Frank Sinatra (kneeling with his eyes shut)

and that in so doing he saved the honor of all of them, she runs after Masterson and admits her love. Later, a Salvation Army officer performs a double wedding—Sarah and Sky Masterson, and Adelaide with Nathan Detroit—as the entire cast ensemble as guests.

To briefly summarize the plot of *Guys and Dolls* is to do it an injustice. It is a character vehicle and its fun and its charm comes from the breezy dialogue and the frantic scurryings of its cast. Almost half of the running time is given over to the songs, all of which set scenes, develop characters and advance the story line. Frank Loesser looked upon *Guys and Dolls* as a musical play and his concept in this and other of his creations was close to operatic. A chronological listing of the songs almost gives away the storyline, from the opening "Fugue for Tin Horns" and "Follow the Fold" to Nathan singing about "Adelaide" and her rejection of him, "Take Back Your Mink," to Sarah's discovery of happiness, "If I Were a Bell," and Masterson gambling with a new-found urgency, "Luck Be a Lady."

Marlon Brando again proved that he could handle any assignment given him. This one was harder than it first seemed, not so much that it was a musical but that the material was very light. Brando wisely played it lightly, almost casually and with no attempt at interpretation. He studied the songs with Frank Loesser and came up with a slim baritone, sufficiently musical but greatly aided by his dramatic ability. Jean Simmons sang with a little more musicality but again it was her delightful acting that carried the part. Miss Simmons is the only actress who has starred with Brando more than once. He had enjoyed working with her in *Desiree* and this helped them to feel at ease with the second job. The enjoyment of their scenes together in *Guys and Dolls* largely comes from his deference to Miss Simmons, he holds himself back in his playing and gives Sky Masterson a tenderness he does not have in the original writing.

Despite the marvelous production values of the film, its fine cast, its musical direction by Jay Blackton, its choreography by Michael Kidd and the sensitive but firm guiding hand of Mankiewicz, *Guys and Dolls* was nowhere near the success Samuel Goldwyn believed it would be. It grossed twelve million dollars, a respectable return for most large-scaled pictures but not enough to move this one into the area of profit. The magic of the stage version dimmed when

transferred to the huge movie screen. The material certainly received all the care and attention and top talent money can buy but as Marlon Brando said to a friend after seeing the picture for the first time, "It's lost its ebullience, hasn't it?"

With Stubby Kaye

With Stubby Kaye, Regis Toomey and Jean Simmons

With Robert Keith, Frank Sinatra, Vivian Blaine, Jean Simmons and Regis Toomey

An MGM Production.
Produced by Jack Cummings.
Directed by Daniel Mann.
Screenplay by John Patrick, from the play by Patrick and the book by Vern J. Sneider.
Photographed in CinemaScope and MetroColor by John Alton.
Art direction by William A. Horning and Eddie Imazu.
Edited by Harold F. Kress.
Musical score by Saul Chaplin, with Okinawan songs written or arranged by Kikuko Kanai.
Running time: 123 minutes.

CAST:

Sakini	Marlon Brando
Capt. Fisby	Glenn Ford
Lotus Blossom	Machiko Kyo
Capt. McLean	Eddie Albert
Col. Purdy	Paul Ford
Mr. Seiko	Jun Negami
Miss Higa Jiga	Nijiko Kiyokawa
Little Japanese Girl	Mitsuko Sawamura
Sgt. Gregovich	Harry Morgan
Mr. Sumata	Minoru Nishida
Mr. Hokalda	Kienzaemon Sarumaru
Mr. Omura	Frank Tokunaga
Mr. Oshira	Raynum K. Tsukamoto

When Marlon Brando heard that MGM had bought the rights to the stage play *The Teahouse of the August Moon* he let it be known that he was eager to play the part of Sakini, the genial, foxy Okinawan interpretor who upsets the U. S. Army's postwar rehabilitation plans for the island. By now Brando's stock was very high, he had won an Oscar and he had proven his dramatic scope. The Kowalski image still hounded

96

THE TEAHOUSE
OF THE AUGUST MOON

(1956)

him but after *Desiree* there was no doubt that he could enunciate beautifully, and with *Guys and Dolls* it was clear that he was an actor capable of almost anything. By 1956 Brando could ask and get any role in any film, and he wanted Sakini. He studied Okinawan speech and body movements and for the actual shooting he subjected himself to a daily two hours of make-up. Brando then played the part so fastidiously that he was barely recognizable as himself, with the consequence that *Teahouse* is not immediately thought of as a Brando film. But it is, and he is its main strength.

In playing Sakini in the film version of the play, Brando denied the part to David Wanye, who had won considerable acclaim with it in the long run on Broadway. The respected and likable Wayne had appeared in a number of films but he had no *pull* at the box office. Once Brando made his bid for Sakini, MGM was not concerned with contenders. It selected Glenn Ford to play the co-starring part of Captain Fisby (John Forsythe had played it on Broadway), and they wisely retained the services of Broadway original Paul Ford as the comically fatuous Colonel Purdy. By the time he stepped before the cameras he had played the part more than a thousand times—and he would play a similarly bumbling, harassed colonel hundreds of times more in Phil Silver's TV series *Bilko*.

As a play *The Teahouse of the August Moon* was a genial satire in an almost fairy-tale mood, its comedy cheerful and deliberately superficial. Its tone was set by Vern Sneider, the author of the novel on which John Patrick based his play, when he said, "The Teahouse was meant to make you think if you want to think and to forget if you want to forget." MGM went along with this concept and decided to make the film an almost literal version of the play. This proved to be

a weakness. Running 123 minutes, almost as long as the play, the film rests too heavily upon its actors and its dialogue. The screenplay was written by playwright John Patrick but MGM might have done better to have assigned a skillful scenarist to help him reshape the material in a more cinematic form.

Basically *Teahouse* is a spoof on bureaucracy, on the military trying to administer local government in an alien culture and being gamboozled by the natives. As in the play, the film opens with Sakini addressing the audience. He introduces himself and the other characters and explains that Okinawa has had the honor to be subjugated by many conquerors, from Chinese pirates in the fourteenth century to American marines in the twentieth: "Okinawa very fortunate. Culture brought to us—not have to leave home for it." He refers to Colonel Purdy, the commanding officer of the occupation forces, as "honorable boss." Purdy is clearly a fussy, officious officer with no understanding of the Okinawans. Captain Fisby arrives on the island and Purdy assigns him to the village of Tobiki, with Sakini as his interpreter, to establish democracy, organize a Women's League, and build a pentagon-shaped schoolhouse—all according to Washington's Plan B.

Captain Fisby is a nice, gentle soul but an unsuccessful officer who has been sent to Okinawa to get him out of the way. The wily Sakini senses the situation. What the village really wants is a teahouse staffed by geisha girls and not a school. Fisby tries to be a firm administrator but he is outsmarted at every turn by the charm of his interpreter. The villagers bring gifts for Fisby, including a beautiful geisha girl named Lotus Blossom. Sakini explains to the flabbergasted captain that he cannot refuse or the villagers will be insulted and difficult to handle. Fisby soon suc-

With Glenn Ford

With Machiko Kyo and Glenn Ford

With Glenn Ford

98

cumbs to the ease of Oriental life, and agrees to the schoolhouse materials being used to build a teahouse. Colonel Purdy becomes confused by the strange line of reportage he gets from Fisby over the phone and fearing that Fisby may have lost his reasoning he assigns an army psychiatrist, Captain MacLean (Eddie Albert) to Tobiki.

MacLean himself is quickly captivated by life in Tobiki. A fanatic on the subject of organic farming he seizes the situation as an opportunity to put his theories into practice with the villagers. He and Fisby attempt to put the village on a profit-making basis by encouraging the citizens to produce handmade wares and sell them to the occupation forces but the scheme falls flat when the villagers fail to make any sales. Depression overcomes Tobiki and Sakini tells Fisby that they will all go home and get drunk. On what? Brandy, replies Sakini, "We make very fine brandy here, from sweet potatoes. Been making for generations." A business boom now overtakes Tobiki, with MacLean on the phone to every army base on the island, placing orders for gallons of local brew.

When the citizens of Tobiki finish their teahouse they invite Fisby and MacLean to a ceremonial party. The festivities are interrupted by an irate Colonel Purdy who orders the building torn down and Fisby placed under arrest. Purdy starts an investigation to find out why nothing has been done about his plans for setting up a democratic government, and why so much money is flowing into the village from the other bases. He assumes, to his horror, that the teahouse is a house of prostitution, and reports his findings to Washington. The reaction amazes Purdy: "Some fool senator misunderstood. He's using the village as an example of American 'get-up-and-go' in the recovery program. The Pentagon is boasting. Congress is crowing." Purdy sinks into a depression, thinking that the villagers have destroyed all their stills and the teahouse but Sakini explains, "We not destroy. Just take away and hide. You watch now, boss." Within an hour Tobiki is reconstructed and Sakini turns to the audience and announces the story is over.

The Teahouse of the August Moon was to have been made in Japan. Producer Jack Cummings

With Glenn Ford

With Eddie Albert, Glenn Ford and Machiko Kyo

With Eddie Albert and Glenn Ford

took his cast and crew and equipment to Japan but left their location near Nara after a few days of shooting because of torrential rainstorms that swamped the area. Recalls Cummings, "Originally the teahouse and garden had been built on a hillside on location. Before the heavy rains arrived we successfully filmed our biggest scenes there, with 250 Japanese farmers from the area as Tobiki villagers. For closer scenes our workers in Hollywood built a remarkable replica of the village at the studio. Incidentally, we brought back the clothes worn by the peasants in the scenes. We couldn't have duplicated them in Hollywood, but I'm sure the farmers were convinced we were crazy when we went around collecting such garments."

The film benefited from the use of authentic Okinawan and Japanese music, recorded in Kyoto and sung and danced by Japanese artists. For the role of Lotus Blossom, Cummings selected Machiko Kyo, who had won acclaim with her dramatic performances in *Rashomon*, and *Gate of Hell*. The lightly comedic part was not only a departure for Miss Kyo but it required her to perform without a knowledge of English. She did it with perfect comic timing and charm. Brando also managed a difficult part with apparent ease, giving correct body movements and vocal inflections and mannerisms, a performance derived from being able to study the Japanese with whom he worked. His roguish Sakini is a delightful characterization.

100

With Paul Ford

With Eddie Albert, Glenn Ford and Paul Ford

A William Goetz Production, released by Warner Bros.
Produced by William Goetz.
Directed by Joshua Logan.
Screenplay by Paul Osborn, based on the novel by
James A. Michener.
Photographed in Technicolor and Technirama by
Ellsworth Fredricks.
Art direction by Ted Haworth.
Edited by Arthur P. Schmidt and Philip W. Anderson.
Musical score by Franz Waxman, incorporating a title
song by Irving Berlin.
Running time: 140 minutes.

CAST:

Major Lloyd Gruver	Marlon Brando
Eileen Webster	Patricia Owens
Kelly	Red Buttons
Nakamura	Ricardo Montalban
Mrs. Webster	Martha Scott
Bailey	James Garner
Hana-ogi	Miiko Taka
Katsumi	Miyoshi Umeki
General Webster	Kent Smith
Colonel Craford	Douglas Watson
Fumiko-san	Reiko Kuba
Teruko-san	Soo Yong

and the Shochiku Kagekidan Girls Revue

Joshua Logan was not only the director of *Say-onara* but he was the man largely responsible for it coming into being. Logan had been fascinated with the culture of Japan and during his first visit to the country in 1951 he happened to meet an old friend, Pulitzer prize-winning novelist James Michener, at the Tokyo Foreign Correspondents Club. Logan exhorted Michener to write a story about modern Japan, one which would allow for a revelation of Japanese theatrical arts. The idea

SAYONARA

(1957)

took root in the mind of Michener and he promised that if a book emerged Logan would automatically have the stage rights to it.

Logan's original idea was to do *Sayonara* as a Broadway musical but legal technicalities arose over the rights to perform the Japanese arts portrayed in the story and Logan then took the property to Hollywood, with the idea of filming it in Japan and using actual Japanese artists in the sections dealing with the country's sacrosanct theatrical traditions. Logan at this time was greatly esteemed for his work as a stage director in New York but he had had no experience with films and there was some doubt about letting him take on a project as complex and as expensive as *Sayonara* looked to be. Logan shelved his Japanese dream for the time being and set about making a film of *Picnic* in 1955 and *Bus Stop* the following year, both of which he had directed in their original stage versions. With the success of these two films Warner Brothers then gave the green light for Logan's filming of *Sayonara*.

Marlon Brando agreed to do the film with little persuasion. He had previously visited Japan and he was eager to return for a closer study of the people and their culture, especially Buddhism and the various oriental philosophies. Brando was also attracted to *Sayonara* because of its emotional plea for racial understanding. By this time it was obvious that the actor's own tastes tended toward the exotic and the liberal. With Brando under contract Warners felt sure of a box officer winner—which proved to be the case— and they invested heavily in the picture. A large company and a great amount of equipment was sent from the Burbank studio in November of 1956 and shooting began the following January. The film involved Logan and his staff for one complete year and it was ready for release, with a running of almost two and a half hours, by the

middle of November, 1957. The trade showings were enthusiastic but there was some comment about its length, with Logan agreeing to a minimal amount of editing, cutting it to 140 minutes.

Sayonara is set in Japan at the time of the Korean War. An American air force ace, Major Lloyd Gruver (Brando) is sent to the air base at Kobe and assigned to light duty as partial recuperation from combat fatigue. Strings have been pulled by his prospective father-in-law General Webster (Kent Smith) in getting him assigned to the Aviation Board, and the general's wife (Martha Scott) and his daughter Eileen (Patricia Owens) arrives from America. Eileen is a sophisticated beauty, much in love with Gruver. He is happy at her arrival but there is some difference in attitude toward the kind of marriage each wants. His doubts are fanned by the character of Mrs. Webster when she demands that her husband reprimand a Marine Captain (James Garner) for trying to bring his Japanese girlfriend into the Officer's Club. Racial tension also comes to Gruver's attention when a tough enlisted airman, Kelly (Red Buttons), a comrade and traveling companion from Korea, ignores his advice and appeals to his Congressman in order to marry his Japanese girl, Katsumi (Miyoshi Umeki). In doing this Kelly is going over the heads of the Far East Command and their refusal to permit marriages between American military personnel and Japanese.

Gruver has no particular feelings about the Japanese, one way or the other, but he accommodates the fascination of his fiancée. They spend an evening at the Kabuki theatre, in which all the roles are played by males, and the meet Nakamura (Ricardo Montalban), a handsome and sophisticated Japanese actor. Eileen and the cultured actor feel an attraction for one another, which is sensed by Gruver, who later quarrels

With Patricia Owens

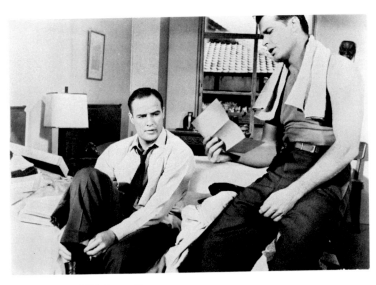

With James Garner

With Miiko Taka

with her about their plans for the future. Gruver agrees to be Kelly's best man at his wedding with Katsumi, and for doing so he is reprimanded by General Webster. Gruver takes the occasion to tell the general that he did not appreciate being pulled out of Korea, and this puts a further strain on his engagement.

Gruver and Marine Captain Bailey run into each other in a bar and then spend an enjoyable time together seeing the sights of Kobe. During their meanderings Gruver catches his first sight of Hana-Ogi (Miiko Taka), the most beautiful of the revered Matsubayashi dancers. These are a group of girls who lead a monastery-like life, dedicated to their craft and denied contact with the public. Gruver is smitten with the girl and spends the following days waiting for the girls to pass on their way to the theatre, in order to see Hana-Ogi, who gradually becomes aware of his attentions. Gruver appeals to Kelly when he learns Katsumi knows some of the Matsubayashi girls, to intercede and arrange a meeting with Hana-Ogi. When she finally comes to dinner at the Kellys' house she admits that she has fallen in love with Gruver. The idyllic match is marred only by their fears of her being found out by her theatre and he by the military. A bigoted colonel (Douglas Watson) finds out about Gruver's romance and brings it to the attention of General Webster. The colonel also initiates an order to ship Kelly and all other men who have married Japanese back to the States without their wives. Eileen becomes aware of all this and realizing she has lost Gruver she goes to the Kelly house and warns the two men of their predicament. Gruver appeals to the general on behalf of Kelly, explaining that Katsumi is pregnant, but he is turned down. He suffers an even greater disappointment when Hana-Ogi tells him she cannot go through with their marriage against American regulations because of the loss of face to Japan.

As a kind of farewell party Gruver and Kelly take the girls to a puppet show, where Japan's famed Bunraku Mitsuwa puppets (almost life-sized) perform "The Love Suicides of Amijima." Returning home the Kellys find their place boarded up and declared off-limits to American personnel. Gruver is placed under arrest. Kelly escapes from the mliitary police assigned to put him aboard his plane, and he and Katsumi return to their home and commit suicide.

Gruver and Captain Bailey discover the

With Miyoshi Umeki and Red Buttons

With Red Buttons

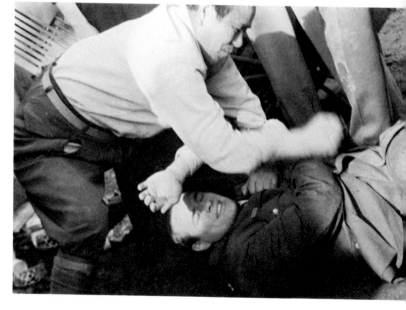

bodies of Kelly and Katsumi, and as they are leaving the house they are set upon by a mob of hoodlums and beaten up. Gruver asks the marine to report the suicide and then goes to the theatre to see Hana-Ogi, but she has left for Tokyo. General Webster is sympathetic and he tells Gruver that a law will soon be passed to allow service-

With Miiko Taka

With Miiko Taka

men to take their Japanese brides back home. Gruver proceeds to Tokyo, to the Matsubayashi Theatre, to see Hana-Ogi. He tells her of his love and asks again for her to marry him. She asks him to wait outside while she decides on her answer. A crowd gathers at the stage door, among them Japanese and American reporters who suspect that the American ace has come to claim Japan's leading dancer. Hana-Ogi appears and announces she has accepted Gruver's offer of marriage, in spite of the criticism it will bring. As the two lovers make their way to a taxi, a newsman asks Gruver if he has a statement for the Far East Command. Replies Gruver, "Tell them 'sayonara' (good bye)."

Sayonara was the commercial success its producers had hoped it would be, although its very commercialism brought murmurs of reproach from the more severe critics. For Brando it was an opportunity to develop and change a characterization while in the course of playing it; his Gruver is a likable but not greatly endearing man as first revealed. It is only when he loves the Japanese girl and becomes aware of the presence of prejudice that he takes on a moral stance and shows concern and courage. The film also allowed Red Buttons, formerly known only as a light comic, to reveal dramatic ability and win an Oscar for his portrayal of the doomed Kelly; his co-player, Miyoshi Umeki, also won an Oscar as the gentle Katsumi. For the part of Hana-Ogi Warners spent a lot of time looking for a suitable, beautiful young Japanese and finally found one at a Nisei exhibition in Los Angeles. Miiko Taka had had no

prior experience in the entertainment business but she nevertheless played the role with charm and credibility.

The technical excellence of *Sayonara* is on the highest level, particularly in its delicate and subtle musical scoring by Franz Waxman, although somewhat hampered by a limp title song from

Irving Berlin. The real value of the film lies in its genuine Japanese settings, lovingly photographed by Ellsworth Fredericks. Much of the footage was taken in Kyoto with generous shots of the giant Buddhas, the Geisha training school, the Bunraku puppet theatre, the Kabuki theatre, and the Imperial Gardens. The exquisite, ancient gardens had, prior to this, been off-limits to film makers.

Joshua Logan and his scenarist, Paul Osborn, wisely balanced the blunt American military opposition to interracial marriage with those of conservative Japanese, equally as opposed. In the final scene it is the young people of Japan who cheer the news of the marriage, not their elders. By 1956 more than ten thousand American servicemen had married Japanese girls, despite the regulations. Presumably, and hopefully, *Sayonara* may one day take its place alongside *Madam Butterfly* in the quaintness of its subject matter.

With Miiko Taka

While on location in Kyoto, Japan, director Joshua Logan and Brando visit the Hogashi Higanji Temple and chat with the high priest

107

A 20th Century–Fox Picture.
Produced by Al Lichtman.
Directed by Edward Dmytryk.
Screenplay by Edward Anhalt, based on the novel by Irwin Shaw.
Photographed in CinemaScope by Joe MacDonald.
Art direction by Lyle R. Wheeler and Addison Hehr.
Edited by Dorothy Spencer.
Musical score by Hugo Friedhofer.
Running time: 167 minutes.

CAST:

Christian Diestl	Marlon Brando
Noah Ackerman	Montgomery Clift
Michael Whiteacre	Dean Martin
Hope Plowman	Hope Lange
Margaret Freemantle	Barbara Rush
Gretchen Hardenberg	May Britt
Captain Hardenberg	Maximilian Schell
Simone	Dora Doll
Sgt. Rickett	Lee Van Cleef
Francoise	Liliane Montevecchi
Brant	Parley Baer
Lt. Green	Arthur Franz
Private Burnecker	Hal Baylor
Private Cowley	Richard Gardner
Capt. Colclough	Herbert Rudley
Corp. Kraus	John Alderson
Private Faber	Sam Gilman
Private Donnelly	L. Q. Jones
Private Brailsford	Julian Burton
Rabbi	Robert Ellenstein
Concentration Camp Officer	Kurt Katch
Medic	Nick King

The Young Lions is a prime example of Hollywood entertainment packaging, put together by solid professionals with all the resources of a

THE YOUNG LIONS

(1958)

major studio at their disposal. This is commercial film making on a high level, a picture designed to appeal to as wide an audience as possible. In its two-and-a-half hours of running time *The Young Lions* covers a wide spectrum of World War Two locations, telling a multiple story and attempting to philosophize about motives and morals on both sides. Under Edward Dmytryk's knowing direction the long and complicated story moves swiftly and logically and includes generous amounts of sex and violence, romance and humor, geography and spectacle. Dmytryk had the aid of an expert team, including two film masters—photographer Joe MacDonald and composer Hugo Friedhofer. Friedhofer here provided what is possibly the finest score ever composed for a war film; its title music, with a hard, relentless drum base, seems to speak of the *business* of war.

Marlon Brando appears in *The Young Lions* as a gentlemanly young German, a presumably idealistic man who embraces Nazism as a pragmatic cure for Germany's problems but who ends his life loathing it. The interpretation differs widely from the original in the Irwin Shaw novel and it caused some controversy. The Brando character, Christian Diestl, spans the entire line of *The Young Lions* but it is interspersed with the stories of two Americans, a lonely Jew, played by Montgomery Clift and a brash Broadway entertainer, played by Dean Martin. The film also deals with the women in the lives of the three men and it is structured in such a manner that there is a linkage between the various characters.

The Young Lions begins in Austria in December of 1938. A young, vacationing American woman, Margaret Freemantle (Barbara Rush) flirts with her courteous and amusing ski instructor, Christian Diestl (Brando) but is disturbed by his sympathy with Nazism. In New York she re-

joins her fiancé, Michael Whiteacre (Martin), a flippant and somewhat irresponsible man with a leaning toward liquor. In a shabby hotel room in California, Noah Ackerman (Clift) visits his estranged father and stays with him as he dies. On the road to Paris in the Spring of 1940 Diestl, now an Army lieutenant, cautions his men about needless abuse of French civilians, a sentiment at odds with the views of his captain, Hardenburg (Maximilian Schell) and Diestl's photographer friend Brandt (Parley Baer), an admitted coward and opportunist.

Ackerman and Whiteacre meet at a draft board. Sensing that he is lonely, Whiteacre invites Ackerman to a party where he meets and falls in love with a young girl from Vermont, Hope Plowman (Hope Lange). In Paris Diestl tries to strike up an acquaintance with a pretty Parisienne, Francoise (Liliane Montevecchi), who keeps him at a distance while Brandt has more success with her friend Simone (Dora Doll). In Berlin Diestl delivers a gift from Captain Hardenburg to his beautiful blonde wife Gretchen (May Britt) and finds her to be a willing subject for seduction. Meanwhile, in America, Ackerman courts Hope and overcomes the objections of her father to their marriage. They decide to marry before he enters the army, while Whiteacre takes an opposite view and tells Margaret they should postpone any thoughts of marriage until after the war.

Diestl and Hardenburg are now with Rommel's forces in North Africa, engaged in pushing the British back toward Egypt. Diestl is a good soldier but he is increasingly bothered by the ruthless attitude of his captain, particularly in the decision to shoot British soldiers rather than take them prisoner. *The Young Lions* is most effective in these African sequences; the battle scenes are brilliantly staged and photographed.

With Barbara Rush

With Parley Baer

With Maximilian Schell

With Maximilian Schell

Ackerman and Whiteacre are placed in the same army barracks and become friends. Ackerman is brutalized by his anti-semitic captain and beaten in a series of fist fights by four husky privates, the last of whom he manages to best. Ackerman then goes AWOL but turns himself in when he learns his wife is pregnant. On returning to the barracks he finds himself accepted by the other men. In Africa the tide turns against the Germans; Diestl and Hardenburg escape from a rout by fleeing on a motorcycle but it hits a land mine. Hardenburg is severely injured, his face almost obliterated, but Diestl is only superficially wounded. In Berlin, Diestl visits his captain in hospital. Hardenburg, his head completely covered in bandages, speaks of his future plans and asks Diestl to call on his wife, from whom he has not heard, and convince her that her husband is "salvageable." He has another request; he points to a horribly burned and mutilated patient in the next bed and reveals that the man has asked Hardenburg to put him out of his misery by killing him. Diestl reluctantly agrees to bring a bayonet on his next visit. When visiting Gretchen Diestl finds her unconcerned, untidy and flirtatious. She tells him that Hardenburg has just killed himself, "with a bayonet." In disgust he knocks her down and leaves.

The disastrous course of the war and the depravity of Nazi behavior cause Diestl to become more and more depressed with his lot as a German soldier. In the fighting in France he sees his regiment cut to pieces and demoralized. He comes across his friend Brandt and the two men make their way to Paris and call upon Françoise and Simone. Brandt tells Diestl that he will desert, marry Simone and become a Frenchman. Françoise pleads with Diestl to follow Brandt's example and desert but this he cannot bring himself to do. He leaves her and promises to return, hoping that a return is possible.

The American armies make their way through Germany. Diestl, now a gaunt, hungry and disheveled wanderer, comes across a concentration camp. The Commandant (Kurt Katch) feeds him and complains about his job—the difficulty of killing six thousand prisoners per day with a staff of only a dozen men. Despair and disgust swamp Diestl and he leaves the camp. As he walks aimlessly around the wooded countryside, totally confused and disillusioned, he smashes his machine gun on a rock and throws it aside. Later as he lies dozing he is awakened by sounds. Diestl

With May Britt

With Liliane Montevecchi, Parley Baer and Dora Doll

looks up and sees two American soldiers, Ackerman and Whiteacre, walking through a clearing. Instinctively he draws his pistol and aims it at the Americans, but he hesitates and decides instead to give himself up. Diestl gets up, fires his gun in the air to get their attention and walks toward the Americans. Confused by the shot and enraged by what they themselves have just seen of the concentration camp, they fire at Diestl. He staggers painfully and slumps to the ground, he breathes a few last, labored gasps and then pitches into a puddle.

Brando dominates The Young Lions with his portrayal of Christian Diestl. His is the agonized Teutonic hero of the kind found in German mythology, and this sympathetic treatment disturbed many people. Critical reaction ranged

111

from those who considered the performance a masterpiece to some who thought Brando self-indulgent and obtuse in his quiet, brooding introspection. *Time*'s reviewer noted: "Brando underplays to the point where in many a scene only a telepathist could hope to tell what he is thinking; but in the long run he imparts an urgent and moving sense that there is a soul somewhere inside the lieutenant's uniform."

Brando refused to play Diestl as written in the novel by Irwin Shaw. He felt that the book had been written while war hatred was still passionate and that by this time, 1958, it would be more interesting to make Diestl a sensitive, doubting Nazi rather than the resolute brute of the Shaw original. Brando prepared a lengthy analysis of the role as he saw it and spent hours reading it aloud to producer Al Lichtman, director Dmytryk and scenarist Edward Anhalt, all of whom had to accede because Fox was eager to have Brando head the cast.

When the company moved to its locations in Paris Brando visited the novelist, who surprised the actor by telling him it was his first contact

With Kurt Katch

112

with anyone involved in the filming of *The Young Lions*. Brando explained the difference in concept over Diestl and asked Shaw if he would have written the part in the same fashion these dozen years after the war. Shaw expressed his low opinion of the German race and said that he doubted if he would modify the character of Diestl. At one point Brando said, "If we continue to say that all Germans are bad, we would add to the Nazis' argument that all Jews are bad." Neither man was able to much convince the other, although they agreed to further debate the issue on television, a plan that unfortunately never came to fruition.

At a press conference in Berlin Brando told a group of reporters, "The picture will try to show that Nazism is a matter of mind, not geography, that there are Nazis—and people of good will—in every country. The world can't spend its life looking over its shoulder and nursing hatreds. There would be no progress that way." A German journalist was moved to comment, "Brando speaks more like a statesman than a movie actor."

With Liliane Montevecchi

A Pennebaker Production, released by Paramount Pictures.
Executive Producers: George Glass and Walter Seltzer.
Produced by Frank P. Rosenberg.
Directed by Marlon Brando.
Screenplay by Guy Trosper and Calder Willingham, based on the novel *The Authentic Death of Hendry Jones* by Charles Neider.
Photographed in Technicolor by Charles Lang, Jr.
Art direction by Hal Pereira and J. MacMillan Johnson.
Edited by Archie Marshek.
Musical score by Hugo Friedhofer.
Running time: 141 minutes.

CAST:

Rio	Marlon Brando
Dad Longworth	Karl Malden
Louisa	Pina Pellicer
Maria	Katy Jurado
Bob Amory	Ben Johnson
Lon	Slim Pickens
Modesto	Larry Duran
Harvey Johnson	Sam Gilman
Howard Tetley	Timothy Carey
Redhead	Miriam Colon
Bank Teller	Elisha Cook
Leader of the Rurales	Rudolph Acosta
Bartender	Ray Teal
Bearded Townsman	John Dierkes
Flamenco Dancer	Margarita Cordova
Doc	Hank Worden
Margarita	Nina Martinez

One-Eyed Jacks is one of the most interesting and peculiar westerns ever made. It is also the only film directed by Marlon Brando, and while it contains many indications of directorial talent, Brando took so long to make it that the film

ONE-EYED JACKS

(1960)

ended up costing three times its original budget. *One-Eyed Jacks* received mixed notices from the critics, most of whom found a great deal to admire and a lot to criticize, and it did only moderately well with the general public. Consequently, the picture never made a profit and Brando has never directed another. But it remains a kind of collector's item among movie buffs, particularly lovers of westerns, because it contains gorgeous photographic sequences of immense, sandy deserts, filmed in Death Valley, and panoramas of the spectacular California coast, near Monterey. It is one of the few westerns to include beach and ocean scenery—a happy inspiration on the part of Brando and another feather in the cap of the much admired cinematographer Charles Lang, Jr. Another of the film's great assets is the musical score of the masterly Hugo Friedhofer, whose composition gives *One-Eyed Jacks* a flow and a feeling it might otherwise not have, since Brando's original print had to be edited by one half. Subtle scoring is a form of invisible mending in film making, and this is a text book example.

One-Eyed Jacks is uneven in its story telling, probably due to the severe editing, but it also has a dichotomy of directorial style. On the one hand it is tough and realistic and on the other it is softly romantic. The picture has excitement and violence, but it is also moody, sensuous and occasionally sado-masochistic. It is difficult not to interpret all of this on a personal level, as a reflection of Brando himself, just as the film's indulgence of its actors with close-ups and lingering reaction shots can only be the work of a director who is himself an actor.

Brando's film is largely a story of vengeance. The story begins with two American bandits operating in Mexico, Rio (Brando), a happy-go-lucky young man who fancies himself as a Ca-

sanova, and Dad Longworth (Karl Malden), an older man looking to end his larcenous ways and settle down. They rob banks with apparent ease and spend their leisure time drinking and courting woman, especially Rio, who has a fondness for aristocratic young ladies; to each he gives his most ''precious'' possession, his mother's wedding ring. This kind of dalliance brings about their downfall. The Mounted Police trail the pair and almost nab them at their lovemaking but Rio and Dad fight their way out and take to their horses, Dad in his stocking feet. The police follow and the bandits are eventually trapped in the desert, with one of their horses shot. Rio and Dad toss a coin to determine who will ride off and who will stay. Dad wins and promises to return with another horse and rescue Rio. Dad also takes the proceeds from their robberies and when he finds another horse at a ranch, he takes it and rides off for the border, leaving Rio to his fate. Rio is captured and spends the years from 1880 to 1885 in the Sonora Federal Prison, until such time as he makes an escape, in the company of a friend, Modesto (Larry Duran).

The embittered Rio is now a man bent on revenge. He finally comes upon Dad Longworth in the town of Monterey, California, and learns that his ex-partner is the sheriff and has taken himself a Mexican wife, Maria (Katy Jurado), with a teen-age daughter, Louisa (Pina Pellicer). Rio rides out to Dad's home, and as Dad recognizes him he prepares for trouble. Instead he finds Rio pleasant and apparently willing to forget past differences. Rio tells him he was never caught by the police, and the guilt-ridden Dad relaxes and invites Rio to meet his family. Rio is in league with two bandits, Bob Amory (Ben Johnson) and Harvey Johnson (Sam Gilman), and they have come to Monterey to rob the bank. His cronies grow impatient but Rio assures them of his in-

With Nina Martinez

tention not only to rob the bank but to kill Longworth at the same time.

Longworth is not completely convinced about Rio and he becomes uneasy when Rio and his step-daughter show a romantic interest in one another. He well recalls Rio's past amorous adventures and he has no wish for anything that will delay Rio in Monterey. The town engages in a fiesta, with the bank not planning to open for several days, and the well-liked, respected sheriff joins the townspeople in their festivities. As Longworth does a Mexican dance Rio regards him from a distance and his eyes betray his loathing. He seduces Louisa as an act of contempt for Longworth but he cannot help but feel tender toward the gentle girl. And it is Rio's soft and chivalrous regard for women that enables Longworth to make his move and rid himself of Rio. In a saloon Rio approaches a drunk mistreating one of the house girls and knocks the man down.

With Karl Malden

With Karl Malden

The drunk then reaches for his gun and Rio draws his own and kills him. Longworth sees his opportunity. He arrests Rio, atkes him into the street, ties him to a horse rail and flogs him with a bull whip. He next takes a rifle butt and smashes Rio's right hand, puts him on his horse and drives him out of town.

Rio and his partners retreat to a small fishing village on the coast; he nurses himself back to health and over a period of a month he practices with his gun, intent on regaining the use of his hand. Amory and Johnson grow impatient and decide to make their own move, and when Modesto refuses to join them, they kill him. Louisa visits Rio at the village. She tells him she is pregnant and he confesses his love for her. But revenge is now even more of an obsession with him and everything else will have to wait. Amory and Johnson fail in their attempt to rob the bank, Rio is blamed and Longworth again arrests him,

With Karl Malden

With Katy Jurado, Karl Malden and Pina Pellicer

117

With Pina Pellicer

this time jailing him and promising him a hanging. Louisa visits him and brings a derringer, and with this Rio is able to overcome the vicious and cowardly deputy, Lon (Slim Pickens). He makes his way to the street, engages Longworth in a gun fight and kills him. Rio says goodbye to Louisa, promises to return and rides away.

The pity of *One-Eyed Jacks*, in many ways a beautiful and entertaining film, is that its production path was so fraught with difficulties, causing a monstrous waste of money over a long period, that it curtailed Marlon Brando's possible career as a director. His behavior on this picture was so obstinate and slow that no studio felt it could risk hiring him as other than an actor. *One-Eyed Jacks* probably sets a gestation-period record for Hollywood films, certainly for a western. It sprang from a meeting between producer Frank P. Rosenberg and novelist Charles Neider in the summer of 1957. Neider had just published *The*

With Slim Pickens and Karl Malden

118

Authentic Death of Hendry Jones and agreed to sell the screen rights to Rosenberg. Both men thought that Marlon Brando would be perfect for the leading role but neither believed the actor would be interested. The first draft of the screenplay was ready by April of 1958 and Rosenberg sent a copy to Brando, thinking that it would be months before he had a reply. Instead he received an enthusiastic call from Brando only three days later, with the usual suggestions for script changes. These changes stretched over the next eight months. Stanley Kubrick, whose first two pictures Brando admired, was hired as director, but he and the actor could not agree on the concept of the characters. After weeks of arguments, Kubrick asked to be released from the engagement. Brando then suggested to Rosenberg that he both star in the film and direct it. Rosenberg was not enthusiastic about the idea, feeling that the project had now become so large it would present a challenge to even an experienced director, but with much money already spent and Paramount breathing down his neck, Rosenberg agreed to Brando as director. Shooting finally started on December 2, 1958.

Producer Rosenberg recalls his experiences working with director Brando: "He pondered each camera set-up while 120 members of the company sprawled on the ground like battle-weary troops . . . every line every actor read, as well as every button on every piece of wardrobe got Brando's concentrated attention until he was completely satisfied. It took six months to film *One-Eyed Jacks* instead of the sixty days for which we had planned. We finished shooting on June 2, 1959. And we took an additional one day —October 14, 1960—to film a new ending. Time and tide are costly in Hollywood, and Brando used both unstintingly in his efforts to get just what he wanted on the screen. He exposed more than 1,000,000 feet of film, thereby hanging up a new world's record. Of this we printed 250,000 feet. (For purposes of comparison, the average important motion picture uses about 150,000 feet of film and prints approximately 40,000 feet of rushes—or original shots). *One-Eyed Jacks* ran four hours and forty-two minutes . . ." Rosenberg and his editors spent months trimming the picture down to two hours and twenty-one minutes, and in their opinion doing it in a manner that did not alter the main story line. Then, after a long post-production period, the film was released in March of 1961, by which time Brando had already made and been seen in *The Fugitive Kind*.

With Karl Malden

With Pina Pellicer

With Ben Johnson

With Pina Pellicer and Slim Pickens

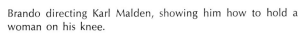
Brando directing Karl Malden, showing him how to hold a woman on his knee.

With Slim Pickens and Karl Malden

Originally budgeted at $1,800,000, Paramount claimed that the final cost of *One-Eyed Jacks* was close to $6,000,000, but just how much of that figure they marked up to studio-overhead we shall never know. We can, however, believe their statement that the film did not make money for the studio.

Marlon Brando has made few comments on this film over the years, allowing only that it was for him a wearying experience, and that he was unhappy about not being able to edit his film. When the film was released he publicly made known his dissatisfaction. Among other things he had been persuaded to change the ending—causing the extra day of shooting more than a year after the rest had been shot. In Brando's version the Mexican girl, Louisa, is killed in the final gunfight, but Paramount considered this down-beat and insisted on at least a semi-happy ending. But for all its problems of production and its failure to make a killing at the box office, Brando's *One-Eyed Jacks*—a title that refers to the duplicity of man—is not a film to dismiss or forget. It lingers in the mind because of its visual beauty and the intensity of some of its scenes, particularly those between Brando and Malden, two knowing actors playing together with the skill of champion chess players. It might be said that the film is rather like the man who directed it—strangely compelling.

Brando directing Karl Malden

A Jurow–Shepherd–Pennebaker Production, released through United Artists.
Produced by Martin Jurow and Richard A. Shepherd.
Directed by Sidney Lumet.
Screenplay by Tennessee Williams and Meade Roberts, based on Williams' play *Orpheus Descending*.
Photographed by Boris Kaufman.
Art direction by Richard Sylbert.
Edited by Carl Lerner.
Musical score by Kenyon Hopkins.
Running time: 119 minutes.

CAST:

Val Xavier	Marlon Brando
Lady Torrance	Anna Magnani
Carol Cutrere	Joanne Woodward
Vee Talbott	Maureen Stapleton
Jabe Torrance	Victor Jory
Sheriff Talbott	R. G. Armstrong
Uncle Pleasant	Emory Richardson
Ruby Lightfoot	Spivy
Dolly Hamma	Sally Gracie
Beulah Binnings	Lucille Benson
David Cutrere	John Baragrey
Dog Hamma	Ben Yaffee
Pee Wee Binnings	Joe Brown, Jr.
Nurse Porter	Virgilia Chew
Gas station attendant	Frank Borgman
Attendant's Wife	Janice Mars
Lonely Girl	Debbie Lynch

Tennessee Williams wanted Marlon Brando for each of his plays after *A Streetcar Named Desire*, and in the case of *Orpheus Descending* he wrote it with Brando and Anna Magnani in mind for the two leading roles. Neither star appeared in the play when in opened in New York in March of 1957; Magnani because of film commitments in

THE FUGITIVE KIND

(1961)

Italy and Brando because he was unsure of the material. He and Williams had conferred many times over the script and it had gone through several versions but none of them convinced Brando. His reservations proved substantial. *Orpheus Descending* closed after a short run on Broadway. Brando later said, "I can tell you why I didn't do it. The Magnani part was great, she stood for something and you could understand her. And Magnani would have wiped me off the stage." Brando felt the part he would have played—Val Xavier—was not well enough defined in terms of what he was for and what he was against, and that Williams could not completely disassociate the actor with *Streetcar's* Kowalski: "He knows I'm the opposite of Kowalski but he still confuses me with the part."

Of all his plays *Orpheus Descending* is the most personal. Says Williams, "Nothing is more precious to anybody than the emotional record of his youth, and you will find the trail of my sleeve-worn heart in this play." The play first appeared in 1940 under the title *Battle of Angels* produced by The Theatre Guild. It was his first full-length work to be professionally staged and it had a very short run. Years later, after the success of *Streetcar, The Glass Menagerie,* and *Cat on a Hot Tin Roof,* Williams was still working on his original play: "A play is never an old one until you quit working on it . . . it never went in the trunk, it always stayed on the work bench." By the time it appeared on Broadway *Orpheus Descending* barely resembled *Battle of Angels,* and when producers Martin Jurow and Richard A. Shepherd approached Williams with the idea of turning the material into a film it was further changed and given another title—*The Fugitive Kind.*

Anna Magnani had won an Oscar for the film version of Williams' *A Rose Tattoo* and readily agreed to this venture. After reading the script Joanne Woodward was so taken with the part of "Carol Cutrere" that she told the producers she would fight to see that no other actress got the role. Williams and the producers then tackled the reluctant Brando, who finally gave in. Whereas Magnani may have "wiped" Brando off the stage, a debatable point, she was not likely to steal scenes from him on the screen, the intimate medium in which his peculiar kind of magnetism has placed other actors in fear of being "wiped out" by him.

The Fugitive Kind is Tennessee Williams' setting of the myth of Orpheus, the artist archetype, descending into hell to rescue Eurydice. As in several of his other plays, Williams' particular hell is a small town in the American South peopled with bizarre characters. His Orpheus is a musical drifter from New Orleans named Val Xavier, who claims that he has been "on a party since I was 15" and is generally sick of his way of life. He is one of the "fugitive kind . . . the kind that don't belong no place at all." At the beginning of the film Val is seen meekly standing before a judge being admonished for his misdemeanors, after which he leaves New Orleans and drives away in his ramshackle car. The car breaks down on the edge of the town of Two Rivers, Mississippi, in a heavy rainstorm, and Val makes his way on foot to the police station. The sheriff is away but his lonely, soft-hearted wife Vee (Maureen Stapleton) offers him food and a bed for the night in a cell. He asks her if she knows of any work in the town and she advises him to apply at the Torrance mercantile store, where she has heard they need a clerk.

Val turns up at the Torrance store wearing his snakeskin jacket (Williams' symbol of the nonconformist) with his guitar on his back and meets Lady Torrance (Magnani), the Italian-born wife of

With Maureen Stapleton

With Joanne Woodward

With Joanne Woodward

With Anna Magnani

124

the owner, Jabe Torrance (Victor Jory), a harsh, bitter man dying of cancer. Lady immediately senses that Val is likely to be a disturbing influence—she, too, is lonely and frustrated—but she hires him. Val very soon comes into contact with yet another hungry woman, Carol Cutrere (Woodward), the drunken, nymphomaniac drop-out of a respectable family. She tries to seduce Val in a cemetery at night but he manages to resist her. The grotesque young lady, a nightmarish Ophelia, tells Val, "I used to be what they they call a church-bitten reformer ... and now I'm not a reformer anymore. I'm just a 'lewd vagrant.' And I'm showing them, showing them all how lewd a 'lewd vagrant' can be if she puts her whole heart in it like I do mine."

When Jabe Torrance returns home from hospital he realizes there is an attraction between his wife and the new clerk. Jabe grabs Lady and pulls her toward him, "I know your plans—I know what your plans are, Lady, but before I go you will be too old for a lover." She replies by telling him she despises him and always has. There is reason for the bitterness between them, and for her hatred of the town. She once bore a stillborn child fathered by a prominent citizen who then deserted her, and her father died trying to save his wine cellar set afire by vigilantes because he sold liquor to Negroes. Lady takes Val to the burned-out building and tells him about the father she loved; "I would sing with my father, we'd wander among the white arbors, him with a mandolin, and me singing. I was beautiful then. I was!" And as she tells him this Val strums his guitar and she begins to sing softly. Lady asks him to live at the store and sleep in the alcove behind the stairs. Instead, he decides to flee the situation. Val takes some money from the cash register for a gambling stake and after winning in a crap game he returns to the store, to get his guitar and replace the money. Lady is waiting for him and calls him a thief. They quarrel but she breaks down and tells him she needs him, and he stays.

Aside from her new-found joy in Val, Lady has plans for expanding the store and building a confectionery, despite Jabe's disapproval. She is determined not to be defeated by him or the townspeople again but while she is away making plans for the opening of the confectionery Val is approached and accused of "messin' with the sheriff's wife." They threaten him with violence if he isn't out of town by the end of the day. The

With Anna Magnani

With Anna Magnani and Joanne Woodward

With Anna Magnani, Virgilia Chew and Victor Jory

With Victor Jory

With Anna Magnani

situation becomes nastier when her husband's nurse (Virginia Chew) tells Lady she knows why Val is leaving—she is pregnant, and not by her husband. Val tells her he must leave but asks her to meet him in some distant place. As they say goodbye, Jabe, in a fit of fury, starts to toss bunches of burning newspapers from his bedroom window down into the confectionery, built by Lady from an arbor. Val rushes into the flames and tries to put them out with his snakeskin jacket, as Lady rushes upstairs to try and stop Jabe. The lovers now meet their death. Lady is shot by Jabe, and the mob of townspeople who turn up at the fire prevent Val from getting out of the burning confectionery. Also at the scene is Carol, who tries to warn Val to get away before the crowd arrives, but he delays himself to find Lady and the delay costs him his life. Later, as Carol walks through the smouldering ruins she picks up the snakeskin jacket and muses, "Wild things leave skins behind them, so that the fugitive kind can always follow their kind."

Marlon Brando's reservations about the material in its original form also, regrettably, apply to the film. *The Fugitive Kind* was not popular with the moviegoing public, and drew a variety of unfavorable comments from the critics. Williams' depiction of the South, however personal, was by now tending to be as ludicrous as it was familiar, and in the case of *The Fugitive Kind* the melodramatic characters defeat the story. It is Williams' contention that hell on earth can be created by the evil men do to one another, but when the villains are as overdrawn as the vicious husband and the brutal sheriff, the absurdly wild Carol and the mean townspeople of *The Fugitive Kind*, the point becomes dulled by gross exaggerations.

The film was made neither in the South or in Hollywood. The producers found a little town in New York State, Milton, which approximated the appearance of a ratty, run-down Mississippi hamlet, and the interiors were shot at the Gold Medal Studios in The Bronx, New York. Sidney Lumet's direction is sensitive and greatly aided by the moody black-and-white photography of Boris Kaufman and the muted, jazzy score of Kenyon Hopkins. The acting is on a high level, with the exception of Joanne Woodward's Carol, so extreme a characterization as to defy playing. Magnani is perfect as the aging, lusty Lady, as is Victor Jory as the malevolent Jabe and Maureen Stapleton as the mousey wife of the sheriff. Stapleton had played the part of Lady in "Orpheus Descending" in the Broadway staging.

To play the sad and wandering Val Xavier, Marlon Brando returned to the image that had dogged him since *Streetcar*, that of the sullen, introspective mumbler, which is possibly a strong reason for Brando's reluctance to play the role in the first place. His acting in *The Fugitive Kind* is mostly subdued, perhaps in order not to suggest any similarity with Stanley Kowalski, but it does have a kind of luminous intensity. His most memorable scene—and this is obviously Tennessee Williams' interpretation of the free spirit of the creative artist—is where he talks about birds that have no legs and spend their lives in the sky because they cannot land: "I seen one once . . . it had a body as tiny as your little finger . . . but its wings spread out this wi-i---de. They was transparent, the color of the sky, and you could see through them . . . But those little birds, they don't have no legs at all, and they live their whole lives on the wing, and they sleep on the wind . . . They just spread their wings and go to sleep on the wind. They sleep on the wind and never light on this earth but one time. When they die."

With Anna Magnani

With R. G. Armstrong

An Arcola Production, released by MGM.
Produced by Aaron Rosenberg.
Directed by Lewis Milestone.
Screenplay by Charles Lederer, based on the novel by Charles Nordhoff and James Norman Hall.
Photographed in Technicilor and Ultra Panavision by Robert L. Surtees.
Art direction by George W. Davis and J. McMillan Johnson.
Edited by John McSweeney, Jr.
Musical score by Bronislau Kaper.
Running time: 179 minutes.

CAST:

Fletcher Christian	Marlon Brando
Capt. William Bligh	Trevor Howard
John Mills	Richard Harris
Alexander Smith	Hugh Griffith
William Brown	Richard Haydn
Maimiti	Tarita
Edward Young	Tim Seely
Matthew Quintal	Percy Herbert
Edward Birkett	Gordon Jackson
William McCoy	Noel Purcell
John Williams	Duncan Lamont
Michael Byrne	Chips Rafferty
Samuel Mack	Ashley Cowan
John Fryer	Eddie Byrne
James Morrison	Keith McConnell
Minarii	Frank Silvera
Graves	Ben Wright
Court Martial Judge	Henry Daniell
Staines	Torin Thatcher
Chief Hitihiti	Matahiarii Tama

MGM's 1962 re-make of *Mutiny on the Bounty* holds a dubious place in film history as a woeful example of a large-scaled production cursed with bad planning and bad luck. The corporate bunglings and indecisions, the artistic temperament and misbehavior of various members of the com-

128

MUTINY ON THE BOUNTY

(1962)

pany, plus sundry unforeseen acts of Nature, caused the film to take twice as long as originally planned and its budget to swell from $8,500,000 to $18,500,000. Since, due to distribution, advertising and exhibition costs, a film must gross more than twice its cost, this picture needed to earn forty million dollars before it could move into profit, a feat so far achieved by less than a dozen films. However, the 1962 *Mutiny on the Bounty* was not quite the financial disaster many people tend to regard it as being. It did gross thirteen million before being sold to television, where showings may bring in a few million more.

This film started out with a problem—the lingering image of MGM's own 1935 version, which won an Oscar as Best Picture of the Year and enormous popularity, particularly for Clark Gable's playing of Fletcher Christian and Charles Laughton's impressive, and much mimicked, characterization of Captain Bligh. The decision to re-do such a highly regarded film as this raised many eyebrows when it was announced, and the first question to come to the minds of movie enthusiasts was: who will play Fletcher Christian? The casting of Marlon Brando met with general approval; some regarded this as an unusual choice—as if it were an invasion of Gable mythology—but there was no doubt that Brando would come up with an interesting account. The end result was not only interesting but greatly surprising; Brando's Fletcher Christian is an aristocrat with a foppish manner and a prissy English accent. This impression of Christian might well be close to the truth but to older moviegoers it was the antithesis of Clark Gable and to younger ones it was so far removed from Brando's Kowalski image as to be amusing. Some critics regard this as one of Brando's most intelligent performances but there are others who feel it tends to be

ludicrous. A few people, perhaps those who own MGM stock, have suggested that Brando's acting in *Mutiny on the Bounty* is a reason for the film not being the great success it was designed to be.

The 1962 film is an expanded version of the 1935 one, allowing for magnificent Technicolor-Ultra Panavision photography, by the esteemed Robert Surtees, of Tahiti and great seascapes, with much more emphasis on what happened to the mutineers after the celebrated take-over of the Bounty. It gives less coverage of Bligh's incredible feat in bringing himself and his eighteen supporters to safety; in actual fact Bligh, in a 23-foot open boat, sailed a distance of 3,618 nautical miles in 41 days in the South Pacific without the loss of a single life. MGM decided not to use the original screenplay but to devise a completely new script, although still sticking as closely as possible to the historical facts. Researchers examined documents at the British Admiralty Library and the National Maritime Museum, and the studio alloted the sum of $750,000 for the building of a replica of the Bounty. The contract was given to the shipbuilding firm of Smith and Rhuland in Lunenberg, Nova Scotia, and they consulted the plans of the original ship. Bligh's vessel was 85 feet long and carried a crew of 62, but the new version was made thirty feet longer to allow for the installation of engines and more deck space for the movement of cameras. The new Bounty made the voyage from Lunenberg to Tahiti, via the Panama Canal, a distance of more than seven thousand miles, in 33 days. It took Captain Bligh more than a year to make the journy from England to Tahiti in his ship.

The story begins in Portsmouth in December of 1787. Captain William Bligh has received orders to sail HMS Bounty to Tahiti to transplant breadfruit plants from that island to Jamaica,

where it is hoped they will serve as a staple in the feeding of plantation slaves. Because of the unusual nature of the voyage, the crew includes a gardener, William Brown (Richard Haydn), somewhat to the amusement of the rough sailors whose quarters he shares. Bligh meets, for the first time, his chief officer, Fletcher Christian and takes an immediate dislike to him. Christian, elegantly attired and arriving at the dock in the company of fashionable friends, is a gentleman

possible time, ignores the advice of Christian and the other officers and sails the ship around stormy Cape Horn, instead of following the prescribed route via the Cape of Good Hope. He does this with the full knowledge that only one ship is known to have made the trip at this time of year and that it cost her half her crew. The Bounty is badly buffeted in the hideously rough seas and a sailor loses his life when a huge barrel breaks loose in the hold. Christian tries to save the man and Bligh objects to him wasting his time when he should be engaged on deck. The rift between the two men grows wider. As a result of being delayed by the stormy seas the Bounty arrives in Tahiti later than planned, at a time when the breadfruit are dormant and cannot be moved. This results in the Bounty having to spend several months in Tahiti, to the chagrin of Bligh but to the delight of his crew. The British sailors are royally received by Chief Hitihiti (Matahiari Tama) and his chief aide, the English-speaking Minarii (Frank Silvera). They stage an elaborate feast, with native dancing, and Christian meets Miamiti (Tarita), the daughter of the chief. The chief expects the officer to make love to his daughter, and—this is one of the few comic moments in the film—Bligh agrees that Christian should indeed 'do his duty.'

With Trevor Howard and Antoinette Bower

With Trevor Howard

with a supercilious manner, the product of a society many stations removed from that of the hard, lonely, earthy Bligh. Christian expresses his disdain for this "grocer's errand" and as the voyage progresses Bligh, a bitterly stern disciplinarian, finds ample reasons to resent Christian. The imperious first officer openly questions Bligh's manner in handling his men, particularly in regard to the flogging of gunner's mate John Mills (Richard Harris) for the stealing of cheese —un unproved charge. Mills, a trouble maker, spots the dissension between Bligh and Christian and tells his shipmates it is something they may use to their advantage in the future. The Bounty, like all ships in the Royal Navy at this time, seethes with the injustice of brutal sailing conditions for the crew.

Bligh, an ambitious career officer eager to win credit for completing his mission in the shortest

With Richard Haydn and Trevor Howard

With Trevor Howard

134

With Tarita

With Tarita

With Trevor Howard and Chips Rafferty

136

With Gordon Jackson, Chips Rafferty, Noel Purcell, Percy Herbert, Frank Silvera, Richard Harris and Duncan Lamont. Kneeling are Richard Haydn and Hugh Griffith

With Richard Haydn

137

With Trevor Howard and Tim Seely

The stay in Tahiti ends and the Bounty is loaded with breadfruit. Once at sea trouble again swells up with Bligh's extreme severity with his men. Christian contains his disapproval but on one occasion, as he gives water to a prostrate seaman, Bligh kicks the ladle from his hand. Christian rebels. He takes a sword and turns on Bligh. This is April 28th, 1789, the day of the mutiny on the Bounty. Most of the crew are for killing the captain but Christian takes command and offers a release for any officer or crewman who prefers not to join the mutiny. Eighteen men elect to leave with Bligh and they are granted one of the lifeboats. As Bligh and his men pull away from the Bounty, the remainder of the crew throw the breadfruit overboard in a frenzy of happiness. But Christian does not share their joy, he realizes the enormity of what he has done and that he will never be able to return to England.

Christian becomes the captain of the renegade warship and he sails her back to Tahiti, there to take on supplies and any of the natives who wish to join them in their new life, including Maimiti. Aware that the Royal Navy will eventually send a party to track them down, Christian tells his men they must find a new home. They settle on the uncharted island of Pitcairn. Time passes and the unhappy Christian points out to the men that they must either return to England or forever remain criminals in the eyes of their government. Few of the men show any interest in returning and the more militant of them make sure that the Bounty will never leave the island. They set fire to the ship, and as Christian rushes into the flames to save the sextant he is trapped by falling timbers and severely burned. Several of the men manage to get him off the burning ship and on to the beach. As the Bounty sinks Christian dies, and his last words to the men are for them to settle their differences and live in peace. At a court martial in England Bligh is exonerated for the loss of his ship, although the Judge (Henry Daniell) takes the occasion to comment on the abuse of rank and the fair treatment of enlisted men.

This version of Mutiny on the Bounty makes for splendid entertainment, even though it can be faulted as being uneven in its writing and its direction. Reaction to Marlon Brando's depiction

138

of Christian must be on a personal basis; it is a highly credible account of a British officer of the period and if the actor's foppish interpretation leaves itself open to some criticism in the early scenes, no such criticism can be laid against his playing of Christian after the mutiny, as the depressed officer broods on his abysmal situation. Brando's playing of the death scene is alarmingly realistic, as he quietly undergoes the agony of Christian's death. Trevor Howard's version of Bligh leaves almost no room for criticism, only the comment that it is very different from the much admired but fruity playing of the part by Charles Laughton. But above all, this *Mutiny* is a magnificently visual film and only the most captious critic could deny the thrilling shots of the Bounty under sail, or the fantastic staging of the storm, and the sequences in Tahiti.

That the film is as good as it is, is something of a miracle in view of the protracted, unlucky and accident-prone period of production. It started out with Eric Ambler as the scenarist and Sir Carol Reed as the director but both Englishmen gave up after months of work because their interpretations were at variance with the concepts of the producer and the head office at MGM. Something of a legend has grown up in Hollywood about Marlon Brando and the part he sup-

posedly played in making things difficult for the production and causing it to be greatly more expensive. Much of this impression was given by an article which appeared in the June 16, 1962, issue of *The Saturday Evening Post*. The article was almost an indictment of Brando and it quoted director Lewis Milestone as saying the actor was responsible for the wasting of six million dollars. The article was strangely biased and contained a number of inaccuracies, including the information that the film finally cost $27,000,000—a mere $8,500,000 more than the actual cost. It allowed Milestone great space in flailing Brando, claiming that he was petty, argumentative and sulking, but it made no mention of the fact that Milestone, occasionally a brilliant director, himself has a reputation for being difficult and, in this case, unsympathetic toward an actor who likes to discuss his parts at length and approach his material carefully.

Marlon Brando was not much interested when producer Aaron Rosenberg first approached him with the idea of playing Fletcher Christian. He later reconsidered and told Rosenberg he might be interested provided the film was not simply a re-make of the former version—which is precisely what MGM had in mind—and that the story be developed after the mutiny to show

With Eddie Byrne, Trevor Howard, Gordon Jackson, Richard Harris and Chipps Rafferty

With Trevor Howard, Gordon Jackson, Richard Harris and
Chips Rafferty

140

With Trevor Howard

what happened to the mutineers. In order to land the actor MGM made this concession and Brando signed a contract early in 1960, with the following October 15th set as the film day of filming in Tahiti. Rosenberg signed Sir Carol Reed and proceeded to London to hire a large British cast. By October 15th, Rosenberg found himself on location with a company of more than a hundred people, at a cost of roughly fifty thousand dollars a day, but with no script and no ship. The Canadian shipbuilders, claiming that the severity of the previous winter caused delays in the delivery of timber, were two months late in launching the Bounty, and Eric Ambler had failed to come up with a script that pleased the producer, Brando, or the head office in Culver City. Ambler threw in the towel and Charles Lederer was brought from Los Angeles to revise and complete the screenplay. Shooting actually began on December 4th but by now Tahiti was in its rainy season and after a few weeks of bad weather the entire company was ordered back to the MGM studios.

Sir Carol Reed resigned, but not, as rumors would have it, because of difficulties with Brando. Reed argued with Rosenberg over the concept of Captain Bligh, whom he didn't want to see played in the Laughton fashion, and Rosenberg further objected to Reed's slow method of filming. Before he left, Reed summoned his cast and explained that his decision to withdraw had nothing to do with Brando. Lewis Milestone was then hired as director, and he and Brando, totally different in temperament and working methods, were at odds all through the production. Shooting was resumed on February 11, 1961, with studio interiors, and the company returned to Tahiti at the end of March. The production dragged on through the next four months, with continual friction over the script, particularly the Pitcairn Island sequence. Brando and Milestone barely spoke to each other and in October, when the final scene—Christian's death —was shot at the MGM studio, Milestone sat in his dressing room as Brando himself directed the shooting. Brando had asked the distraught and harassed Rosenberg if he might look at the film and after doing so he suggested that the ending be re-shot. Rosenberg eagerly agreed and Brando filmed the sequence at no charge to the studio for his own services.

Mutiny on the Bounty, running one minute less than three hours, took most of 1962 to edit and package, and it was released in November of

that year. Having heard so much about its production problems, many critics seemed eager to
look for faults but almost all agreed that it was a
handsome film to look at. The mixed reaction to
Brando may have been influenced by the general
feeling in the film industry that his alleged misbehavior was responsible for the fearful cost of
the picture. A similar feeling was directed shortly
after toward Elizabeth Taylor and the forty million dollars spent on Cleopatra. In both cases the
gossip smacked of an industry looking for scape-
goats. So widespread was this sentiment that
MGM president Joseph Vogel was moved to
make a public announcement praising Brando
for his cooperation during the long filming and
placing the blame on accidents, bad weather, ill-
nesses and various misunderstandings. Rosenberg has admitted: "Marlon gave us a rough
time, but he felt we were not living up to the
agreements we made with him about the basic
concept of the picture."

Shortly after the film was released Marlon
Brando revealed his own views on the troubles
of Mutiny on the Bounty. He told Dave Jampel of
Variety: "If you send a multimillion dollar production to a place when, according to the pre-
cipitation records, it is the worst time of the year,
and when you send it without a script, it seems
there is some kind of primitive mistake. The reason for all of the big failures is the same—no
script. Then the actor becomes the obvious target of executives trying to cover their own
tracks." Brando admitted that the article in The
Saturday Evening Post had caused him trouble,
especially from MGM stockholders, accusing him
of unprofessional conduct. He denies the
charges or: "It's all so simple. If an actor was working for me and got out of line, I'd get the Screen
Actor's Guild on the phone. They have the authority to punish actors. They've done it before."

With Sandra Church

A Universal Picture.
Produced and Directed by George Englund.
Screenplay by Stewart Stern, based on the novel by
William J. Lederer and Eugene Burdick.
Photographed in Eastman Color by Clifford Stine.
Art direction by Alexander Golitzen and Alfred Swee-
ney.
Edited by Ted J. Kent.
Musical score by Frank Skinner.
Running time: 120 minutes.

CAST:

Harrison Carter MacWhite	Marlon Brando
Deong	Eiji Okada
Marion MacWhite	Sandra Church
Homer Atkins	Pat Hingle
Grainger	Arthur Hill
Emma Atkins	Jocelyn Brando
Prime Minister Kwen Sai	Kurrit Pramoj
Joe Bing	Judson Pratt
Rachani	Reiko Sato
Munsang	George Shibata
Senator Brenner	Judson Laire
Sears	Philip Ober
Sawad	Yee Tak Yip
Andrei Krupitzyn	Stefan Schnabel
Colonel Chee	Pock Rock Ahn

Marlon Brando, ever the political idealist,
began to speak of using film as a medium for social comment almost as soon as he established
himself in Hollywood. *Viva Zapata!* appealed to
him because of its glorification of a revolutionary; he thought at the outset that *The Wild One*
would give some understanding of rebellious
youth, and he felt *On the Waterfront* had some-

THE UGLY AMERICAN

(1962)

thing to say about corruption in trade unionism. *Sayonara* was a plea, albeit highly romanticized, for racial tolerance, and *The Young Lions* allowed Brando to theorize about the Nazis. Long enchanted with the culture and the philosophy of the Far East Brando took a trip to Southeast Asia in 1958 with the idea of trying to find a story that would point up the United Nations technical-assistance program. He said at the time, "I feel this is an enormous and singular step forward in the history of human relationships because for the first time in the world we have people of diverse natures, colors, religions, points of view and philosophies working together for the common good of mankind."

nothing in terms of film came from Brando's trip and it was not until four years later that a viable Southeast Asia story came into his view. At that, it was not a case of Brando finding the story, it was brought to him in screenplay form by producer George Englund, a man two years younger than Brando, who then read the entire script aloud to the actor. Brando made an immediate decision to film *The Ugly American*.

As a novel by William L. Lederer and Eugene Burdick *The Ugly American* had been widely read and discussed. Its very title had been a subject for discussion among Americans—why, with all the vast and generous aid the United States had heaped upon the world, were Americans regarded as ugly? This intrigued Marlon Brando, who had discovered a few of the answers on his overseas trips: "For all our incredible facilities for modern communication, we have communicated very little with the world. I think we are insulated. I've seen Westerners in Thailand, in Java, in Japan, and most of them make no effort to learn the language or participate. They have their air-conditioned offices and Scotch in their ice boxes. They bring in a little society of America to

the place they live in." These points are part of the thematic material of *The Ugly American*, the first American feature film, couched as entertainment, to deal with American foreign policy in Asia.

The film is set in the mythical country of Sarkhan, a country fraught with factional disputes, an opposition to American aid and a Communist party struggling to gain control. To Sarkhan comes the newly appointed United States Ambassador Harrison Carter MacWhite, formerly a newsman specializing in southeast Asian affairs, who has won his post over the objections of several members of the Senate Foreign Relations Committee. They are concerned about his friendship with Deong (Eiji Okada), the revolutionary responsible for Sarkhan's independent spirit. Arriving in Sarkhan with his wife Marion (Sandra Church) and his chief aide, Grainger (Arthur Hill), MacWhite is given a ceremonious greeting which quickly disintegrates into an anti-American riot. MacWhite's main plan in placating the Sarkhanese is to enlist the aid of his friend Deong but this becomes a questionable course when he learns that Deong is negotiating with the Communist leaders. MacWhite visits Deong, who introduces him to his wife Rachani (Reiko Sato). The friendship between the two men crumbles when Deong voices his opposition to MacWhite's pet project, the Freedom Road, which the ambassador feels will help the people in their economic growth. Deong believes, as do the Communists, that the highway serves the purpose of the military and the monopolistic government of Premier Kewn Sai (Kukrit Pramoj), regarded by Deong as an American puppet.

MacWhite visits the site at which the Freedom Road is being built and meets the supervising engineer, Homer Atkins (Pat Hingle) and his wife Emma (Jocelyn Brando). The ambassador is im-

With Arthur Hill and Sandra Church

With Arthur Hill

With Eiji Okada

pressed with the work being done by the Atkins
couple in operating a clinic for orphaned children, which he rightly regards as being both hu-
mane and diplomatic, but he disagrees with the
engineer over the course of the highway. Mac-
White feels the road should run directly north
into the Communist controlled part of Sarkhan.
He persuades Kwen Sai of this and promises
American military aid should there be interven-
tion from foreign powers. On learning of this
Deong openly aligns himself with the Communists and leads a revolt against the government.

On the occasion of Sarkhan's anniversary of
independence MacWhite proposes a state cele-
bration at the construction headquarters on the
Freedom Road. The revolutionaries seize the occasion to make an attack. Saboteurs blow up the
construction camp and its fuel tanks and raze the
children's hospital. MacWhite visits Kewn Sai to
try and clarify the situation and the premier
shows him proof of Communist involvement and
that he will have to admit defeat in the face of a
regime led by Deong. Kwen Sai also reveals to
MacWhite that he has discovered, from captured
officers, a plot to assassinate Deong and use him
as a Communist martyr. MacWhite sees this as a
chance to save Sarkhan. He tells Deong of the
plot. The rebel leader refuses to believe it but investigation confirms the treachery. Deong agrees
with MacWhite that he must join forces with
Kwen Sai in order to save the country from a for-

With Eiji Okada and Reiko Sato

147

With Eiji Okada

With Pat Hingle, Sandra Church and Jocelyn Brando

With Arthur Hill

eign takeover but as he is about to leave his headquarters Deong is fatally shot by his aide Sawad (Yee Tak Yip), a Communist officer. Deong lives long enough to tell his people of their real enemies and to remove the stigma of imperialist from his friend MacWhite. However, MacWhite realizes, despite his good intentions, he has bungled his schemes and he resigns his post.

The Ugly American ends on a bitter and trenchant note. MacWhite gives a press interview and it is carried on network television in the United States. He tells the reporters, and the public, that in order to help the countries of Southeast Asia, "we must understand their internal problems before inflicting our way of life on them. We can't hope to win the cold war unless we remember what we're for as well as what we're against." He condemns Americans for their complacency and indifference, and as he does so a man watching the broadcast in his home reaches towards his TV set and flicks it off. The bored, unconcerned viewer has not been able to find anything *interesting* to watch.

Unfortunately the final shot in *The Ugly American* proved indicative of public reaction. The film was not the success Brando and George Englund hoped it would be. It was considered commendable in its intent but many critics found it a little dull and labored. Brando was admired for his sincerity, for doing something that he felt was worth doing but the general public was possibly confused by the complexities of the politics of the mythical nation. The long film, a solid two hours, could not have appealed to the unsophisticated since the decent motives of its ambassador hero result in chaos. In view of all that has happened in Vietnam since the film was made, *The Ugly American* is now not only outdated but somewhat quaint in its earnest simplicity. Nonetheless, its humanistic view points are still apropos.

Universal gave the picture considerable production value. They sent a photographic unit to Thailand for three months to gather background footage of the countryside and of Bangkok, and establishing shots of government buildings, schools and temples. An Asian village of some thirty acres was built on the studio's backlot, plus several elaborate sets on sound stages, representing an expenditure of around half a million dollars. Courage was also shown by the studio in the casting. Japanese actor Eiji Okada was brought in to co-star with Brando in the role of

Deong. Okada had come to international attention through his appearance in *Hiroshima, Mon Amour* but he had never appeared in an American film and he knew very little English, which somewhat hampered his performance in *The Ugly American*. An influential Thailand newspaper publisher named Kukrit Pramoj, who had also served as his country's Minister of Finance, was hired as the film's technical consultant but he so impressed Brando and Englund with his personality that they persuaded him to take the role of Kwen Sai, the Sarkhanese premier.

Brando admits *The Ugly American* was not as effective as it might have been but he feels it had, and has, value as a comment on the hypocrisies and dangers of blind political doctrine. His fascination with the Far East and the Orient has increased with the years, especially on the philosophical level. Brando warns Westerners that their material wealth has little meaning for East Indians: "What you are as an individual, what your particular philosophy is, what your manner is, how you deport yourself are also very strong considerations in their acceptance of you."

With Sandra Church

A Lankershim–Pennebaker Production, released by Universal Pictures.
Executive Producer: Robert Arthur.
Produced by Stanley Shapiro.
Directed by Ralph Levy.
Screenplay by Stanley Shapiro and Paul Henning.
Photographed in Eastman Color by Clifford Stine.
Art direction by Alexander Golitzen and Robert Clatworthy.
Edited by Milton Carruth.
Musical score by Hans J. Salter.
Running time: 99 minutes.

CAST:

Freddy	Marlon Brando
Lawrence	David Niven
Janet	Shirley Jones
Fanny Eubank	Dody Goodman
Andre	Aram Stephan
Colonel Williams	Parley Baer
Mrs. Sutton	Marie Windsor
Miss Trumble	Rebecca Sand
Miss Harrington	Frances Robinson
Sattler	Henry Slate
Dubin	Norman Alden
Anna	Susanne Cramer
Frieda	Cynthia Lynn
Hilda	Ilse Taurins
Gina	Francine York

Bedtime Story was Marlon Brando's first fling at broad film comedy and he was able to prove that clowning was well within his range. Many critics felt the material was beneath his talent but there were others who felt that it was something of a relief to see Brando being an amusing ham and thereby departing from his image as an intense dramatic actor. The public reaction to the

BEDTIME STORY

(1964)

picture was generally good but the story line was far too lightweight and incredible to make a great change of direction in Brando's career. *Bedtime Story* is engaging hokum only at the time of being watched, any afterthought quickly dispels it as shallow. It is, in fact, a typical Universal Picture of its time, expertly packaged by a team of creators long versed in facile screen comedy, seemingly sexy, supposedly sophisticated but actually as contrived a product as breakfast cereal. Its writers, Stanley Shapiro and Paul Henning, are Hollywood veterans in the art of glib-witty situation comedy; Henning, among many successes, originating the long-running TV series *The Beverly Hillbillies*, and Shapiro, who also produced *Bedtime Story*, had established himself at Universal with such winners as *Pillow Talk*, *Operation Petticoat*, and *That Touch of Mink*, and this film is clearly cloth from the same tailor.

The film rests squarely on the talents of Brando and David Niven, and while it was something of a surprise to see Brando being so pleasingly comic, it was expected that Niven would carry off the role of gentleman farceur as he had done many times before. Here the two men are both tricksters, each a confidence man preying on women but each a vulture of different stripe. Niven poses as a prince, a charming but impoverished member of European royalty and Brando is an Army corporal given to nefarious dealings and seduction of girls by epic lies. When first seen Brando, as Freddy Benson, takes an instant photograph of a German cottage and after having placed the photo in his wallet he knocks on the door of the cottage and explains to the lone inhabitant, a lovely young lady, that he is in the area trying to locate the birthplace of his grandmother. The girl is aghast when shown the photo, she reveals to the mock-amazed Benson

that he is in the very house he is seeking. The subsequent tour of the premises ends in the bedroom. Benson's photo trick, oft repeated, finally lands him on the carpet before his colonel, who is himself bamboozled into giving Benson a hushed-up discharge (plus money) when he discovers his daughter is one of Benson's victims and that his regiment is rife with illicit dealings masterminded by Benson.

On a train going from Germany to the French Riviera, Benson comes across Lawrence Jamieson, a seemingly conservative gentleman who expresses amazement at Benson's knowledge of the foibles and weaknesses of women. Jamieson palms himself off as an old-fashioned married man, whereas an early sequence in the film has established him as a trickster who woos contributions from rich American widows and heiresses to support his "kingdom" and save his "people." Jamieson, in fact, lives in palatial comfort on the Riviera, his redeeming feature being his support of several local artists and artisans. Spotting Benson as possible competition, Jamieson arranges for a young lady to whisk him off to Italy but it is a ruse that fails and Benson soon sizes up Jamieson's true place in the scheme of things. Rather than be revealed, Jamieson agrees to taking Benson as a partner. Their partnership is successful and Benson is particularly useful when posing as the moronic, demented younger brother of the "prince." Whenever the subject of marriage arises between Jamieson and one of his wealthy victims, exposure to the young brother soon has the intended bride retreating from the alliance.

The Jamieson-Benson partnership undergoes a strain with the arrival of a pretty young American girl named Janet (Shirley Jones), whom they are told is a "Soap Queen." With both men attracted to Janet they enter into a contest to see which

With Susanne Cramer

With David Niven

With David Niven and Frances Robinson

152

With David Niven and Frances Robinson

With Shirley Jones
and David Niven

153

With Shirley Jones

With David Niven
and Shirley Jones

154

With David Niven

With Shirley Jones

one will first be able to pry from her the sum of twenty-five thousand dollars. Benson's ploy is to climb back into his corporal's uniform and place himself in a wheelchair as a psychosomatic cripple, a man stricken with paralysis after learning of the infidelity of his girlfriend, who "ran off with a dancer." He quickly wins the sympathy and the affection of the soft-hearted Janet. Jamieson allows himself to be known as an eminent and expensive Swiss psychiatrist, the one Benson has been writing to in the hope of getting an appointment, one he knows he can't possibly afford.

The two men try to outwit one another, with Benson at a disadvantage since he has to operate from a wheel chair, but the tenor of the game changes when they learn that Janet is not rich but simply a working girl who has won a beauty contest. Jamieson, by far the more scrupulous of the pair, decides to back off but Benson, ever lecherous, remains bent on seduction. He succeeds in his quest but loses the contest by falling

in love with Janet and offering to marry her. On the boat back to America she speaks of the job her father has arranged for him and the apartment her mother has picked out for them and to all her remarks he meekly replies, "Yes, dear." Presumably the trickster has been trapped and will now conform to domesticity, chastened and happy.

The ending of *Bedtime Story* is implausible. Nothing about Benson as played by Brando leads one to consider him redeemable. Niven's Jamieson is much more believable, his is a cultured cad of some compunction. Jamieson might well be *Raffles* twenty-five years later. However, it is not a film to be taken seriously although had it been produced a few years later it would have been held in contempt by the Women's Liberation movement—and justly so. Here all the women are soft and gullible, all of them prone to male charm. Only in a male flight of fancy could women be so pliable and so easily seducible, so usable and so discardable.

An Arcola-Colony Production, released by 20th Century–Fox Film Corporation.
Produced by Aaron Rosenberg.
Directed by Bernard Wicki.
Associate Producer: Barney Rosenzweig.
Screenplay by Daniel Taradash, based on the novel by Werner Joerg Luedecke.
Photographed by Conrad Hall.
Art direction by Jack Martin Smith and Herman A. Blumenthal.
Edited by Joseph Silver.
Musical score by Jerry Goldsmith.
Running time: 128 minutes.

CAST:

Robert Crain	Marlon Brando
Captain Mueller	Yul Brynner
Esther	Janet Margolin
Colonel Statter	Trevor Howard
Kruse	Martin Benrath
Donkeyman	Hans Christian Blech
Dr. Ambach	Wally Cox
Branner	Max Haufler
Milkereit	Rainer Penkert
Baldwin	William Redfield
Admiral	Oscar Beregi
Nissen	Martin Brandt
Ensign Sloan	Gary Crosby
Kurz	Charles De Vries
Busch	Carl Esmond
Wilke	Martin Kosleck
Steward	Norbert Schiller
German Crew Member	Robert Sorrells
Crew Member	Rick Traeger
Lt. Brandt	Ivan Triesault
Commander Kelling	Robert Wilke

The fact that Aaron Rosenberg hired Marlon Brando to head the cast of *Morituri* belies some-

MORITURI

(1965)

what the tales of tension between the star and the producer during the making of *Mutiny on the Bounty*. On the other hand it is ironic that this film should also be a nautical yarn dealing with strife aboard ship and that in making it the company should run into some of the same stresses and strains that plagued *Bounty*. Brando did not get along well with German director Bernhard Wicki, largely because both men are perfectionists but unsympathetic toward each other's idea of arriving at perfection. Brando has always been a slow and meticulous actor, never ready to approve a scene unless he considered it correct, and yet he was intolerant of Wicki's similar attitude, complaining that the director would take as many as twenty attempts to bring off a scene. At the outset of production Rosenberg and his staff explained to Twentieth Century–Fox that the long and complicated story would take ninety days to film but the studio ordered the film shot in sixty days. As a consequence *Morituri* ran over its budget and beyond its schedule and proved to be a harrowing experience for Bernhard Wicki, who was here exposed to the Hollywood system for the first time. Wicki had distinguished himself in Germany with his film *The Bridge* but his style of film making was greatly at variance with the California film factories. Wicki has been used to being the head man on his team, working with a small crew and taking his time. Now he had a Front Office breathing down his neck, constantly reminding him that millions of dollars were at stake. Nonetheless, the talented Wicki was able to give the picture dramatic tension and a strange moody quality.

Morituri is very much a German story. The book on which it is based was written by Werner Joerg Luedecke, who was a German naval attaché in Tokyo during the second World War,

until it was discovered that he was partly Jewish. He was then sent back to Germany on a freighter, virtually a prisoner, and ended up in a punishment battalion on the Russian front. Much of the material in *Morituri* is inspired by his own experiences, and to achieve a true feeling of authenticity Rosenberg decided to bring in director Wicki and several German actors.

The story begins in the summer of 1942 when German merchant naval Captain Mueller (Yul Brynner) is called to the German Embassy in Tokyo and ordered to sail a freighter, with a strategic cargo of rubber, to occupied France. He balks at the assignment; he is himself apolitical but his first officer, Herbert Kruse (Martin Benrath), is a fervent Nazi and his crew includes civil and political prisoners. His prediction of disaster is overruled. Meanwhile, a British Intelligence Officer, Col. Statter (Trevor Howard), approaches a rich and sophisticated young German living in India, Robert Crain (Brando) and inveigles him, with threats of exposure to the Nazis, into working for the British. Crain's mission is to pose as an SS Officer and sail on Mueller's ship as an observer, and at the same time facilitate the British capture of the ship. Crain's primary task is to disarm the explosive charges by which the ship is to be scuttled in the event of capture, thereby keeping its vital cargo out of the hands of the enemy.

In accepting the job Crain takes his leave of the British Intelligence Officer with the words of the Roman gladiator's chant: "Morituri te salutant" (We who are about to die, salute you). On board the freighter, the Ingo, the Captain makes known his disdain for Crain, considering him a spy sent to watch him, and Crain quickly makes an ally of Kruse, telling him he may need him should it be necessary to take command of the ship. The ruse is onerous to Crain, whose views

157

With Trevor Howard

With Yul Brynner

158

With Yul Brynner

are actually the opposite of those of Kruse and more in line with those of the captain, whom he respects. He tricks Kruse into revealing the location of the scuttling charges, and later disconnects them, all except one in the refrigeration hold. The freighter comes close to being scuttled when it emerges from a fog bank and finds itself close to a British convoy but an attack by Japanese submarines engages the attention of the British and the Ingo slips away. Later, one of the submarines arranges a rendezvous with Mueller and eighteen American naval captives and one German Jewish girl, Esther Levy (Janet Margolin) are transferred. Crain enlists the aid of Esther, revealing himself in his true light. He asks her to rally the Americans into a mutiny to help him take over the ship but the only way she can persuade them is to offer herself as a prostitute to the whole group.

Crain is soon after revealed in a radio broadcast as an Allied agent. Among the men on board sides are drawn but the sailors loyal to the Nazi cause are better organized and armed and the mutiny is put down. Among the victims is Esther, brutally beaten and shot by Kruse. Crain escapes the confusion and confronts Mueller in his cabin; he tries to persuade the captain to resume command of his ship rather than let Kruse take over. Mueller refuses and Crain decides to scuttle the ship. The crew abandon the slowly sinking freighter and on deck Crain and Mueller face each other, both puzzled by the other's philosophy: Crain by Mueller's service to a cause he despises and Mueller by Crain's paficism turned to violence. Inadvertently Mueller spots a few barrels of lard in the refrigeration hold where the single activated scuttling charge had blown. He plugs the hole in the hold in the hope that the ship may last a while longer. Crain then asks Mueller to radio an allied ship in the area; he is at first reluctant to do this but as the film ends we hear the click-click of a radio key over a shot of the ruined vessel.

Morituri was not a success at the box office

159

With Yul Brynner and Martin Benrath

With Yul Brynner, Janet Margolin and Wally Cox

160

With Yul Brynner

With Janet Margolin

and once more Brando was chided by the critics for appearing in a film that did not advance his career. It is a peculiar film, seemingly a wartime action yarn but actually an attempt at something deeper. Brilliantly photographed in black-and-white by Conrad Hall and subtly scored by Jerry Goldsmith, the picture swirls with psychological undercurrents and moral equations. It's strength is also its weakness; *Morituri* attempts to deal honestly with Germans of the Nazi era and tries to shed a sympathetic light on those who were anti-Nazi and those who are generally referred to as *good* Germans. For American and British film makers this has yet to prove a commercially rewarding exercise. Brando ran against this problem with *The Young Lions* in trying to present a Nazi officer in something other than shades of evil. In *Morituri* his anti-Nazi is civilized and decent but such is the structure of the film that he is forced into the hero's spotlight. British Intelligence is presented as unscrupulous in blackmail-

162

ing the Brando character into serving its cause and the American seamen prisoners are despicable in their treatment of the Jewish girl. Their gang rape is not far removed from the kind of experience the girl would have received from the Nazis. While these situations may actually be close to the truth it nonetheless diffuses the emotional impact on the audience, especially an audience whose anti-German sentiment has long been fanned by Hollywood itself.

The effort put into the making of *Morituri* was considerable. The script called for a vintage freighter of the kind that would have been pressed into service as a blockade runner in the second World War. Producer Rosenberg and his staff finally found a suitable subject, a 540-foot vessel built in Scotland in 1938 and resting in Yokohama harbor, the Blue Dolphin. They chartered the Chinese-owned ship to their shooting location, the waters of Catalina Island, some twenty miles south of the Fox studios in Beverly Hills. The studio also spent $80,000 building a plywood replica of a Japanese submarine. Most of the film was shot at sea, with admirable realism backing up its arresting but disturbing storyline.

An Horizon Picture, released by Columbia Pictures.
Produced by Sam Spiegel.
Directed by Arthur Penn.
Screenplay by Lilliam Hellman, based on the novel and play by Horton Foote.
Photographed by Joseph La Shelle.
Art direction by Robert Luthardt.
Edited by Gene Milford.
Musical score by John Barry.
Running time: 135 minutes.

CAST:

Sheriff Calder	Marlon Brando
Anna Reeves	Jane Fonda
Bubber Reeves	Robert Redford
Val Rogers	E. G. Marshall
Ruby Calder	Angie Dickinson
Emily Stewart	Janice Rule
Mrs. Reeves	Miriam Hopkins
Mary Fuller	Martha Hyer
Damon Fuller	Richard Bradford
Edwin Stewart	Robert Duvall
Jason Rogers (Jake)	James Fox
Elizabeth Rogers	Diana Hyland
Briggs	Henry Hull
Mrs. Briggs	Jocelyn Brando
Verna Dee	Katherine Walsh
Cutie	Lori Martin
Paul	Marc Seaton
Seymour	Paul Williams
Lem	Clifton James
Mr. Reeves	Malcolm Atterbury
Mrs. Henderson	Nydia Westman
Lester Johnson	Joel Fluellen
Archie	Steve Ihnat
Moore	Maurice Manson
Sol	Bruce Cabot
Slim	Steve Whittaker

THE CHASE

(1966)

Mrs. Sifftifieus	Pamela Curran
Sam	Ken Renard

Sam Spiegel is among the most astute and respected American producers. He was responsible for *On the Waterfront, The African Queen, The Bridge on the River Kwai,* and *Lawrence of Arabia.* His filmic concepts run to the grand and the noble, and that is possibly why *The Chase* is such a lamentable disappointment. It is a small story made gargantuan and the end result of all the time, effort and money spent on it is hideous exaggeration. With a director like Arthur Penn, a writer like Lillian Hellman and a large, impressive cast *The Chase* should have been a profitable venture, or at least a critical success. As it was, the critics were almost unanimous in angrily flailing the picture because of its sordid account of life in a present-day small town in Texas. Pauline Kael called it a "liberal sadomasochistic fantasy," and several critics pointed out that had the film shown black southerners as it does white—as vicious, bigoted and sinful—it might well have provoked a civil rights reaction. Set in a fictional town called Tarl, *The Chase* spends more than two hours revealing a morass of alcoholism, adultery, brutality and fanaticism. Only the sheriff is decent, and the townspeople lift not a finger to help him. In this respect it is rather like an updated version of *High Noon* in a *La Dolce Vita* framework.

The film has its origin in a book and play written by Horten Foote. The play appeared at New York's Playhouse Theatre in April of 1952 and lasted less than a month. It was directed by Jose Ferrer, and John Hodiak played the sheriff—Marlon Brando's part in the screen version. Despite Brando's top billing, the part of the sheriff is relatively small. *The Chase* is a conglomerate story

but principally that of Bubber Reeves (Robert Redford), sent to a penitentiary on what may have been a false charge, who escapes and makes his way home. He and a fellow escapee seize a car and kill the occupant, although the killing is actually done by the companion, who then makes off with the car and leaves Bubber to take the blame. It is the news of his return that sets Tarl spinning; this is the kind of town so popular in American fiction, a town more or less ruled by one man—Val Rogers (E. G. Marshall), a land baron and banker around whose neck the economy of the town seems to hang. Bubber's wife, Anna (Jane Fonda), is having an affair with Rogers' son Jake (James Fox), who also happens to be Bubber's best friend. All of this makes Tarl uneasy about Bubber coming home, particularly on a wild Saturday evening when most of the population seem to be attending noisy, drunken parties, the largest of which is being thrown by Val Rogers and attended by all the "in" people.

The gossip and the speculations about the return of Bubber act as a catalytic force on the lives of several people in the town, many of whom think him a dangerous criminal and a few who consider him innocent, including sheriff Calder (Brando). The sheriff is generally thought to be in the pay of Rogers but he isn't, and it is Rogers who is most concerned about Bubber's arrival. Rogers, despite his wealth and power, has reason to be afraid. A number of people would like to tell Bubber that his wife is Jake's current girl-friend. Calder's wife Ruby (Angie Dickinson) tries to persuade him to steer clear of the coming trouble but the sheriff feels he must do his duty. Among the less than admirable citizens is Emily Stewart (Janice Rule), the bored wife of Rogers' vice-president Edwin Stewart (Robert Duvall), an apparent nymphomaniac who openly admits her affair with her husband's colleague, Damon

166

With E.G. Marshall and Angie Dickinson

Fuller (Richard Bradford), whose own wife, Mary (Martha Hyer) has been driven to drink by her cruel, unloving husband. Stewart and Fuller despise their employer and plan his downfall, in a manner that will enable them to take command of his businesses.

Sheriff Calder is beaten by Stewart and Fuller, as a warning for the lawman to keep away from the situation. The beating makes Calder even more intent on his duty. Jake, who shares the general hatred for his father, and Anna set out to find Bubber and protect him from the various people who would like to see him dead. They wrongly assume the sheriff is one of them, and the sheriff assumes the same of them. When Bubber reaches Tarl he hides in an automobile junk yard on the edge of the town, and he sends a black friend, Lester Johnson (Joel Fluellen), to find Anna and bring her to him. Johnson is seen entering Anna's apartment by Fuller and a pair of drunken cronies, and they are prepared to beat him, claiming that as a black he has no business with a white woman, when Calder arrives on the scene and saves him. Calder puts Johnson in jail

for his own safety but Rogers arrives and persuades the black man to reveal Bubber's hiding place. At the junkyard Rogers finds his son and Anna with Bubber, and he tries to get Jake away from the scene with the promise of helping Bubber. But it is too late—dozens of drunken townspeople turn up at the dump with the idea of ferreting out Bubber and enjoy themselves doing it. They light gasoline bombs (bottles with cloth wicks) and hurl them into the dump and send burning tires spinning through the wrecked cars. Jake is fatally wounded by an explosion and Bubber is saved from lynching by Calder. But the next day, as Calder leaves the jail with Bubber to take him to a safer place, one of the townspeople steps forward and kills Bubber with gun shots.

The Chase is admirable on the technical level, especially its scenes in the junkyard as the frenzied mob hurl their gas bombs through the night air, but it is outrageously melodramatic. It is an incredible web of enmities and jealousies, handsomely staged and acted with gusto but as a comment on American Life *The Chase* gives

167

With Angie Dickinson

168

much reason for concern. If Tarl is to be believed it is also to be avoided; at one point the sheriff says to his wife, "Some of those people out there are just nuts," and it is such an understatement as to be amusing. The scene in which Bubber is shot down by an assassin—not in Horton Foote's original—is so obviously inspired by the Jack Ruby killing of Lee Harvey Oswald that it is in shocking bad taste. Just why the picture is so intensely exaggerated is hard to ascertain; the producer and the director have complained about pressure from the gentlemen in the front office of Columbia Pictures, to make the drama exciting and explicit in order to protect the heavy investment. This may be so but it doesn't completely condone Sam Spiegel and Arthur Penn.

Lillian Hellman receives full and single credit for the screenplay of *The Chase* but in an interview with Irving Drutman, published in *The New York Times* of February 27, 1966, she revealed that the picture was not only a great disappointment to her but that the screenplay as filmed was not what she intended: "Decision by democratic majority vote is a fine form of government,

With Miriam Hopkins

With Joel Fluellen

but it's a stinking way to create. So two other writers were called in, and that made four with Mr. Spiegel and Mr. Penn, and what was intended as a modest picture about some aimless people on an aimless Saturday night got hot and large . . ."

Brando's Sheriff Calder is a normal, decent-minded man and almost an oasis amid the miserable, cowardly citizens of the town. He plays it in his usual studied manner, adopting a genuine Texas accent—something many of the other actors don't do—but the part as written and directed is somewhat ambiguous. Brando has been an outspoken critic on violence and corruption in American life and it is easy to see why he was interested in playing the part. That he was not completely successful was not entirely his fault.

For their book *The Director's Event* authors Eric Sherman and Martin Rubin interviewed Arthur Penn and, in discussing *The Chase*, mention was made of Sheriff Calder being the only really adult figure in the story. Said Penn: "He was a man whose whole action in the picture was to hold on to a mature view and avoid an infantile, retaliatory aggressive stance. He had to try and cool it as best he could in a community which was somewhat infantile in its views. The sadness of the story is that Calder failed. The other sadness is that we failed Calder. We failed Brando because we didn't dramatize that nearly well enough, and that to me was the conspicuous failure of the film. Calder was an interesting character with a fascinating motive, but we stepped all over our feet trying to get that on the screen."

170

With Angie Dickinson

With Robert Redford

A Universal Picture.
Produced by Alan Miller.
Directed by Sidney J. Furie.
Screenplay by James Bridges and Roland Kibbee, based on a novel by Robert MacLeod.
Photographed in Technicolor by Russell Metty.
Art direction by Alexander Golitzan and Alfred Sweeney.
Edited by Ted J. Kent.
Musical score by Frank Skinner.
Running time: 98 minutes.

CAST:

Matt Fletcher	Marlon Brando
Trini	Anjanette Comer
Chuy Medina	John Saxon
Lazaro	Emilio Fernandez
Squint Eye	Alex Montoya
Ana	Miriam Colon
Paco	Rafael Campos
Ramos	Frank Silvera
Priest	Larry D. Mann
Yaqui Woman	Argentina Brunetti

Marlon's Brando's second film venture into the Wild West bears some similarity with his first but it is, regrettably, far less interesting and effective. Like *One Eyed Jacks*, *The Appaloosa* is set in the Mexican border country in the latter part of the nineteenth century and tells of a loner on the trail of revenge. The two pictures also share the distinction of highly artistic color photography, in fact, it is the camera work of Russell Metty that gives *The Appaloosa* its only real quality. Metty had by this time in his career been a photographer for thirty years; among his credits are such handsome pictures as *Spartacus*, and *The War Lord*. *The Appaloosa* presents frame after frame

THE APPALOOSA

(1966)

of gorgeous southwestern landscapes in tastefully set technicolor. Unfortunately, photographic effect runs to excess and this is not so much the fault of Metty but director Sidney J. Furie, a Canadian who achieved his first major success in England with *The Ipcress File*. Furie's fussy, modish film technique was well suited to the "Swinging London" setting of the spy thriller but in this, his first Hollywood project, his indulgences flooded the picture. Huge close-ups of faces, parts of faces and bodies, spurs, bottles, fires and grillwork all tend to deflect attention from the story rather than aid it.

The Appaloosa also suffers from a painfully slow treatment of its slim material, with its characters allowed to leisurely reveal themselves. The project obviously started out with the idea of being a quality product and an attempt to enlarge the canvas of the traditional western. This is what drew Brando to the film, the idea of authenticity in telling a western story, and not the usual, fanciful yarn. In playing an aging saddle tramp named Matt Fletcher, Brando was trying to portray a western Everyman. The result is far too subjective, possibly because the very mannered actor was up against a very mannered director.

The title of the film refers to a select breed of horse, with distinct markings, somewhat like a pinto, and having special characteristics. It is the one cherished possession of Matt Fletcher, a weary wanderer, a buffalo hunter by trade, who wants to settle down and breed appaloosas. After avenging the murder of his Indian wife, Fletcher comes to the border town of Ojo Prieto. He enters a church and prays, hoping to unburden himself of his past life and his sins and start anew. But such is not to be. As he prays, his prize horse is stolen by a lovely young woman, Trini (Anjanette Comer), who is desperate to escape her boyfriend, Chuy Medina (John Saxon), a

handsome and aristocratic bandit chief with a sadistic streak in him. She tells Chuy that Fletcher has molested her and as he enters the church to confront the gringo, off she rides. She is soon captured and returned by Chuy's men. Chuy is struck with the idea of owning the magnificent horse and he offers to buy it. Fletcher refuses, despite the ominous reception the refusal receives from the bandits, and he rides off to visit his friends Paco (Rafael Campos) and Ana (Miriam Colon), a young married couple with two children, who run a farm in the desert. On the way he is set upon by Chuy and his men, who humiliate him and drag him by rope through a rocky stream, as Chuy makes off with the Appaloosa.

Fletcher recuperates with his friends. Once his health is restored he sets out to revenge himself and reclaim his horse. He rides across the border and visits Chuy's headquarters in Cocatlan, where he challenges the bandit to personal combat. This gesture is accepted but the contest is an unusual one—Indian hand wrestling with poisonous scorpions on either side, ready to sting the hand that is lowered. It is Fletcher who loses and the bandits leave him to die. He saves himself by gouging out the poison with a piece of broken glass, after which Trini, now sympathetic toward him and even more bitter about Chuy, helps him to reach a ramshackle hut owned by an old farmer, Ramos (Frank Silvera), where he slowly recovers. Again he ventures into the bandit stronghold and this time not only retrieves his horse but takes Trini with him. She has, we discover, been sold to Chuy by her parents and has hated his brutal, possessive treatment. By now, Trini and Fletcher have become appreciative of one another. Two of Chuy's men track Fetcher to the home of Ramos, and in a gunfight he kills the two bandits, with Ramos being a sideline victim. Fletcher and

With John Saxon

With Anjanette Comer and Rafael Campos

176

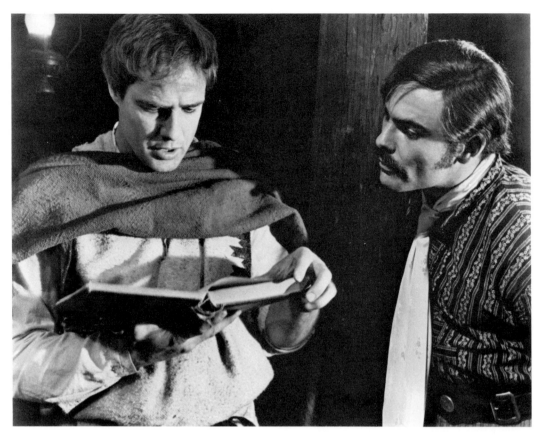

With John Saxon

With John Saxon

177

Trini head for the border but before they reach it Chuy and his chief henchman, Lazaro (Emilio Fernandez), catch up with them and trap them in the rocks on a mountainside. After Fletcher kills Lazaro, Chuy calls to him and explains he will leave Fletcher alone if he will hand over the girl. Fletcher looks at Trini and realizes she means more to him than his horse. He sends the Appaloosa running out and as Chuy fires at the horse a glint of sunlight on his rifle reveals his position. Fletcher takes careful aim and mortally wounds Chuy, and when the bandit dies the two ride off into the distance for their new life together.

The Appaloosa was a failure as a theatre attraction and when released to television its impact was further diminished by the loss of clarity in the one area in which the film excelled, its scenic photography. The director's gimmicky style is even more irksome on TV, with its rest-less camera focusing on objects in the foreground of its actors, in its reflected shots and its complicated frames. To Furie's credit the film does have a sense of hidden danger, of violence under its beautiful, quiet surfaces, and his actors are excellent, particularly John Saxon as the wicked, smiling Chuy. But it is the Brando characterization that dominates the picture; it is another of his brooding, tortured, simple men, and, as in so many of his other films, a man suffering brutal physical treatment. There was a difference of opinion between the star and the director over the matter of interpretation of the leading role, causing some strain during production. Some time later, when Brando ran into the director on a street in London he greeted him affably and said that they must "do it again sometime." Mr. Furie replied that he didn't think it was very likely.

A Jerome Epstein Production, released by Universal Pictures.
Produced by Jerome Epstein.
Directed and written by Charles Chaplin.
Photographed in Technicolor by Arthur Ibbetson.
Art direction by Bob Cartwright.
Edited by Gordon Hales.
Musical score by Charles Chaplin.
Running time: 108 minutes.

CAST:

Ogden Mears	Marlon Brando
Natasha	Sophia Loren
Harvey Crothers	Sydney Chaplin
Martha	Tippi Hedren
Hudson	Patrick Cargill
Miss Gaulswallow	Margaret Rutherford
John Felix	Michael Medwin
Clark	Oliver Johnston
The Captain	John Paul
The Society Girl	Angela Scoular
Steward	Peter Bartlett
Crawford	Bill Nagy
Saleswoman	Dilys Laye
Baroness	Angela Pringle
Countess	Jenny Bridges
Immigration Officer	Arthur Gross
French Maid	Balbina
Hotel Receptionist	Burnell Tucker
Purser	Leonard Trolley
Electrician	Len Lowe
Head Waiter	Francis Dux
Photographer	Kervin Manser
Nurse	Carol Cleveland
An Old Steward	Charles Chaplin

Marlon Brando had said early in his film career that the two film makers he most admired were

THE COUNTESS FROM HONG KONG

(1967)

Elia Kazan and Charlie Chaplin, a choice too obvious to need much discussion. But whereas the esteem for Kazan grew from their work together, Brando's regard for Chaplin, like that of most everyone, rested on a body of work far in the past. When Chaplin announced he wanted to make another film and that he thought Brando would be excellent as the male lead, the actor accepted without first seeing the script, assuming that anything by Chaplin would be worth doing. Of all Brando's pictures *The Countess from Hong Kong* is the most difficult to review because there is so little say about it. It is a feeble, threadbare, pitifully old fashioned bedroom farce. Bosley Crowther in his review for the *New York Times* summed up the feelings of most critics in saying, ". . . if an old fan of Mr. Chaplin's movies could his charitable way, he would draw the curtain fast on this embarrassment and pretend it never occurred."

A charitable view of Chaplin's career would be to consider *Limelight* (1952) as his last film. He was then sixty-three and had been in Hollywood for almost forty years. *Limelight* was a poignant, personal film with much to say about the joys and sorrows of being an entertainer, and it had the makings of the perfect swan song. He came out of his retirement in Switzerland five years later to make *A King in New York,* a mildly amusing comedy but so anti-American in tone it has never been released in the United States. Almost a decade passed before he ventured into the film world again, obviously moved by the need to make one more, last picture. The idea of *The Countess from Hong Kong* had come to him while making a trip to Shanghai in 1931; he sketched it out as a possible movie project and put it away. Some years later he considered it as a vehicle for himself and his then wife Paulette Goddard but it never came to fruition. Even as a

picture made in the 1930's it would have been dated, and as a film of the mid-1960's it is a sad absurdity. Its concept and its antics belong in the kind of film Chaplin made in his early, silent period, and as such it would probably have been delightful.

The film begins in Hong Kong as an American millionaire-diplomat named Ogden Mears (Brando) enjoys himself in a night club, prior to sailing the next day on a liner to America. He enjoys the company of a number of attractive young ladies, the most prominent of whom is the Countess Natasha (Sophia Loren), a Russian emigré of no means. She explains she has made a living since the age of thirteen as a dance-hall girl. With the ship at sea the next morning, Mears discovers Natascha hiding in his stateroom. She is determined to get to America and she threatens to brand him an abductor if he reports her as a stowaway. Mears, taking a world cruise to recover from an illness, almost has a relapse when he receives word he has been appointed American ambassador to Saudi-Arabia. Already harassed by a wife who wants a divorce, the poor man now has to deal with a voluptuous woman hiding in his quarters. The journey from Hong Kong to Honolulu turns into a series of frenzied attempts to conceal Natascha everytime someone comes to his cabin, which is often. Mears soon lets his secretary Harvey Crothers (Sydney Chaplin) and his manservant Hudson (Patrick Cargill) in on his dilemma and enlists their aid.

With Natascha, beautiful and helpless, running around in his pajamas and constantly popping in and out of closets, romance inevitably overcomes the pair. In order to give the girl national status Crothers suggests that Hudson marry her, with the understanding that as an American citizen she will be able to get a passport in Hawaii, as

With Sophia Loren

With Sophia Loren

182

With Sophia Loren

With Sophia Loren

With Geraldine Chaplin

well as an immediate divorce. The marriage is performed by the ship's captain, with further comic complications arising from the groom not being able to share his bed with his bride although having to give the impression he is. When the ship docks in Honolulu Ogden's wife Martha (Tippi Hedren) comes aboard to affect a reconciliation with her husband and proceed with him to his new appointment. Natascha escapes the ship by dressing as an Hawaiian and diving overboard. Within a little while of being with his wife Ogden decides that he does not want to resume the marriage and that Natascha is more important to him than his career. And he races after her to find her and tell her so.

The meagre plot of *The Countess from Hong Kong* is spread over two full hours and Chaplin's direction can only be described as pedestrian. Much of the story takes place in the stateroom during the voyage across the Pacific but there is so little sense of motion it might well be in an hotel. The film occasionally comes to life with the furtive dashing around to hide the girl from visitors but it becomes repetitious. Chaplin's tendency toward bathroom humor is here overdone, as Brando is required to loudly belch after taking an Alka-Seltzer, not once but several times, and at one point a radio is turned up to hide the sound of someone using the toilet. A few good moments are scored by the actors,

With Bill Nagy, Kervin Manser and Sidney Chaplin

With John Paul, Sydney Chaplin and Tippi Hedren

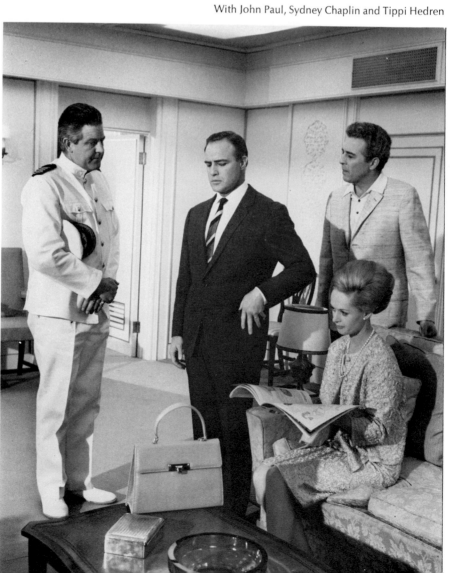

principally the late Margaret Rutherford in a vignette as a daffy and crotchety bed-ridden passenger, and Patrick Cargill as the put-upon manservant, married to a magnificent female and allowed to sleep in the next bed but denied all access. Chaplin himself provides one of the highlights in a brief appearance as a seasick old steward. Would that he appeared more. The two stars struggle against impossible odds, having been given shallow characters to portray and ludicrous lines to speak, such as, "You won't believe me when I tell you this is the first real happiness I've known."

For Brando *The Countess from Hong Kong* was a distressing experience and by the end of production he was barely on speaking terms with his former idol. Perhaps the saddest thing about the film is Chaplin's adamant defense of it. He took the critical trouncing very badly: "If they don't like it, they're bloody fools. Old fashioned? *They* are old fashioned . . . I'm not worried. I still think it's a great film, and I think the audiences will agree with me rather than the critics." Unfortunately, such did not prove to be the case.

With Charles Chaplin

With Sophia Loren

A John Huston-Ray Stark Production, released by Warner Bros.–Seven Arts.
Produced by Ray Stark.
Directed by John Huston.
Screenplay by Chapman Mortimer and Gladys Hill, based on the novel by Carson McCullers.
Photographed in Technicolor by Aldo Tonti.
Art direction by Bruno Avesani.
Edited by Russell Lloyd.
Musical score by Toshiro Mayuzumi.
Running time: 109 minutes.

CAST:

Leonora Penderton	Elizabeth Taylor
Major Weldon Penderton	Marlon Brando
Lt. Col. Morris Langdon	Brian Keith
Alison Langdon	Julie Harris
Anacleto	Zorro David
Stables Sergeant	Gordon Mitchell
Capt. Weincheck	Irvin Dugan
Susie	Fay Sparsk
Private Williams	Robert Forster

The novels of the late Carson McCullers were often referred to as being Southern Gothic, in which the American South became a weird netherland of the mind, its horror stemming from the spiritual torments of Miss McCullers' characters. Such material is exceedingly difficult to transcribe into film because its sly introversions and its symbolism, open to all kinds of interpretations, elude the firm point of view so necessary in telling a story on the screen. In making *Reflections in a Golden Eye*, John Huston wisely chose to treat the strange tale and its group of grotesque characters in a straightforward manner, almost as if they were not grotesque. The film is admirable in many ways, beau-

REFLECTIONS IN A GOLDEN EYE

(1967)

tifully staged and photographed and splendidly acted but Huston and his company are defeated by the McCullers characters—they are figments of abstruse dreams, best left to the imagination of readers than to the observations of viewers.

Huston begins the film with a simple statement lifted from the first page of the McCullers' novel: "There is a fort in the South where a few years ago a murder was committed." He repeats that statement at the end of the film, immediately after the murder has occurred and it is the nature of that murder that supplies the gist and the color of the story. There are six main characters: Major Weldon Penderton (Marlon Brando) and his wife Leonora; their next-door neighbors, Lt. Col. Morris Langdon (Brian Keith) and his wife Alison (Julie Harris); the Langdons' Filipino houseboy Anacleto (Zorro David); and a young soldier, Private Williams (Robert Forster). The time is late 1948 and the setting is a U.S. Army post in Georgia, bordering on a forest preserve.

Private Williams, who works in the stables and has great sympathy for horses, is ordered to report to the Penderton home, where the Major instructs him to clear away some underbush in his backyard. The Major's manner is peremptory, as if trying to play the role of martinet rather than actually being one. It is an authoritarian front masking a devious, insecure, impotent man. Penderton's relationship with his attractive, lusty wife is seemingly nonsexual; she finds an outlet for her earthy, vital nature in an adulterous affair with Langdon, carried on almost openly. Leonora also gives vent to her physical energy in a passion for horses and riding, she is attached to a handsome white horse she calls Firebird and she taunts her husband by telling him that the horse is indeed a *stallion* and an animal with the soul of a gentleman. Leonora is confident and arrogant, an army brat who has grown up on military

posts and she despises her husband's lack of virility. He in turn regards her as a vulgarian.

The Pendertons and the Langdons socialize frequently. Alison, a frail and neurotic woman, is well aware of her husband's affair with Leonora. She has been ill since the death three years earlier of a malformed baby and more recently she has tried to mutilate her breasts, partly from grief and a feeling of maternal failure and partly as punishment from her husband's infidelities. Alison's only sense of well being comes from her close friendship with her houseboy, Anacleto, an elfin, effete companion who shares her interest in music and art and is in every way the opposite of her brusque, burly husband.

Private Williams, a sullen, lonely man, is fascinated by the fiery Leonora and her occasional kind comments to him. He takes to visiting the Penderton house at night and peering in the windows. He observes Leonora in the nude, presumably his first such experience, but he also observes the Major in his study. In what is a cruel but trenchant invasion of privacy Williams—and the audience—learns disturbing things about Penderton. The Major is a latent homosexual, who finds torment in marriage and who yearns for his early years as a young soldier and its simple masculine comradeship. He is also a fetishist who slyly hides things in boxes in his desk; we see him gazing at a photograph of a Greek male sculpture and we watch as the Major unwraps a spoon he has stolen from a fellow officer.

Leonora and Langdon often ride together and on one occasion Penderton joins them. He is an inept horseman, to the disdain of his wife. The three of them spot another rider cantering around a field. It is Private Williams and he is completely naked. Leonora and Langdon laugh and move on but Penderton continues to look, he expresses disgust but there is something in his

190

With Elizabeth Taylor and Brian Keith

With Elizabeth Taylor

With Elizabeth Taylor

look that betrays a fascination. Late that night Private Williams enters the Penderton house and sneaks to the room of Leonora. He spends the night squatting by her bed, fondling her clothes and staring at her. With the dawn he gets up and returns to his barracks but he is seen by Alison. She brings it to Leonora's attention, who dismisses the information as another sign of Alison's dementia, and borrows Anacleto to help with the preparations for a party she is giving. On the night of the party Penderton decides to take Leonora's horse out for a ride and prove to himself he can master the animal. He fails to do this; Firebird bolts and Penderton loses control and falls from the horse after a long and furious ride. In a fury of anger he takes a stick and savagely flails the horse. Humiliated and hurt Penderton both cries and laughs at his experience; usually unemotional in company he now allows himself to express emotion. He assumes he is alone but he isn't; Private Williams, who has been sunbathing, appears on the scene, stark naked, and quietly leads Firebird away. Arriving home with his clothes torn and his face cut and scratched Penderton receives sympathy from his wife, until she learns he has injured her horse. She then takes a riding crop and in the presence of her guests she whips it back and forth across Penderton's face.

Penderton begins to grow fascinated with Private Williams. Lecturing to military students in a classroom his attention is deflected by the sight of Williams through a window. Days later, when giving another lecture, Penderton speaks glowering but haltingly about the value and the strength of leadership in an officer, and it becomes apparent that he is tragically lacking in the qualities he fervently admires. His life now becomes tortuous on two levels—his craving for Williams and the strife in his home when Alison claims that the private is spending the nights with Leonora in her room and thereby deceiving both Penderton and Langdon. No one believes her and Langdon comes to the conclusin he must commit his sick wife to a sanitarium. Within a few days of her commitment Alison dies of a heart attack.

Leonora and Langdon find it difficult to con-

192

tinue their passion now that his wife, formerly a rationalizing subject for discussion between them, has gone. Penderton continues to stalk Williams; he follows him from a distance and on one occasion he picks up a candy wrapper Williams has dropped and adds it to his collection. Penderton seems to come to terms with his real nature; in a discussion with Langdon and Leonora he speaks in favor of the fey, disappeared Anacleto, whom Langdon claims would have been better off in the army and toughened up. Asks Penderton: "Is it better, because it is morally honorable, for the square peg to keep scraping around the round hole rather than to discover and use the unorthodox square that would fit it?"

The strain begins to show on Private Williams, a man, it is revealed, who has been put off women by his father. Williams is sexually frustrated but the object of his desire is Leonora and not the Major. He gets up in the night and makes his way through a rain and lightning storm to the Penderton house. Penderton spots him as he looks from his window at the storm; he turns off his light and sits on the edge of his bed, nervously straightening his hair in eager anticipation of a visit. But he waits in vain. Williams creeps by and enters Leonora's bedroom. He holds a piece of her lingerie as he kneels by the side of the soundly sleeping woman. Penderton, his eyes blazing with anger, enters the room with a pistol in his hand. The two men look at each other for a moment, then Penderton raises the pistol and fires several shots. Williams falls dead as Leonora wakes, screaming with confusion and terror.

Reflections in a Golden Eye is an engrossing film but not a pleasing one. It is faithful to the spirit of the McCullers original but it leaves some doubt about purpose and about conclusions. The strange sextet of characters are neatly tucked away on a remote army post and the film therefore becomes a comment on a particular way of life rather than on life itself. It questions hypocrisy and the so-called normalcies of society but it suggests the price of abnormalcy is hideously high. Producer Ray Stark has called it a film about "the underworld of your mind." In doing so he supposes, at considerable commercial risk,

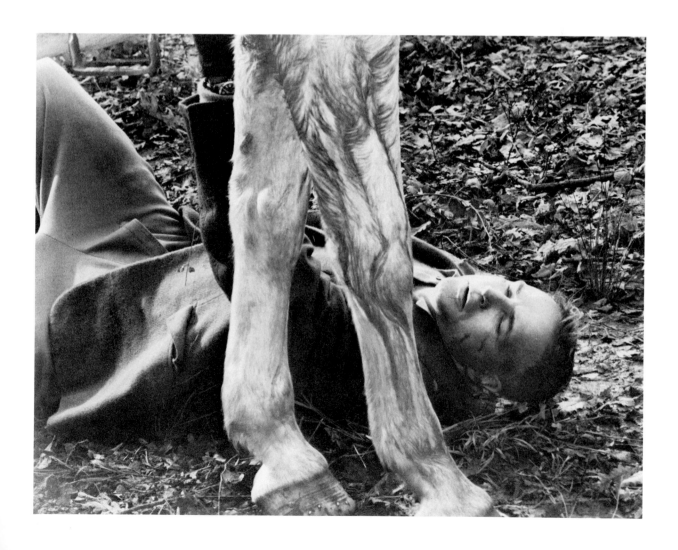

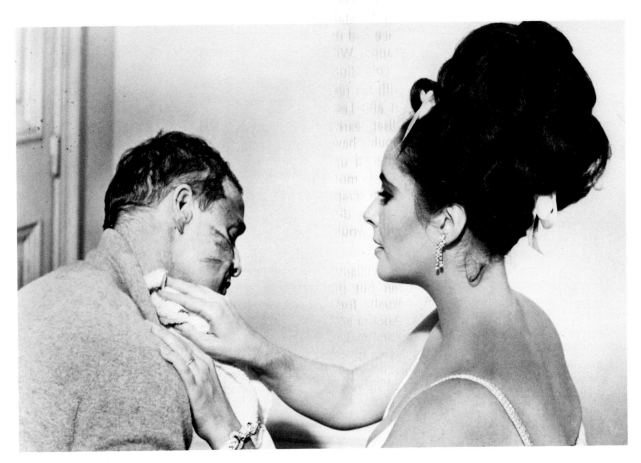

With Elizabeth Taylor

that wide audiences will care to admit to such thinking. Within a few months of the film's release it was clear to Warner Brothers, and to Stark and Huston, that they had miscalculated in assuming that the popularity and power of Elizabeth Taylor and Marlon Brando would clear the difficult subject matter at the box office.

There is much to admire in *Reflections in a Golden Eye* as the work of top flight film makers and a few things to deplore. Much of the film was made in Italy, at the Dino De Laurentiis Studio and on countryside near Rome, with two weeks of locations on Long Island, New York, to get authentic army base backgrounds. Filming an American story in Europe may have accounted for the film's rather remote feeling. Also on the negative side of the ledger was Huston's decision to use severely muted color stock, giving the picture a faded sepia look but also giving it a melodramatic pretentiousness the bizarre story cannot support. Neither can it support a musical score, by Toshiro Mayuzumi, that telegraphs the actions of the actors. But it is the acting that makes *Reflections in a Golden Eye* a film worth

seeing. Elizabeth Taylor is precisely right as the luscious but shrill and insensitive wife, as is Julie Harris as the addled Alison. Brian Keith, an actor always better than his material, here has a part he does justice. John Huston gambled on two newcomers for Private Williams and the effeminate Anacleto, and in the gaunt Robert Forster and in New York hairdresser Zorro David he found the ideal images. From Marlon Brando Huston pulled one of the most complex and subtle performances the actor has ever given on the screen.

Brando's Major Penderton is a man living in a pitiful twilight zone. He is a dreadfully lonely man who slowly realizes his homosexual nature and agonizingly becomes aware of a general weakness in his very being, that he is not the man he should be in order to hold the rank and position he has. A strange mixture of prissiness and martial authority, Penderton lives a tormented, shadowy existence. Brando's moments alone on screen reveal the fissures in the man with astonishing honesty. We see him building up his muscles with weight lifting and afterwards flexing his

muscles in the mirror. Several scenes with mirrors divulge the private Penderton: he stands and salutes himself, he scowls with disapproval one moment and smiles with satisfaction the next. Later, as he thinks of the young soldier, he plies his face with his wife's rejuvenating cream. Brando's Penderton is a helpless, crippled but graceful human, and as played by him the part calls not for sympathy but for understanding. It is a portrait of a cold and isolated man and Brando delineates him with his stance, his walk, his eyes and the muscles of his face. Again Brando assumes a southern accent and although he can be criticized for garbling some of his lines, and a few crucial ones are completely lost, it is the voice and the speech pattern of a thwarted and unhappy man.

With Elizabeth Taylor and Robert Forster

A Co-Production of Selmur Pictures (Hollywood), Dear Films (Rome) and Corona Films (Paris), released in the U.S. by Cinerama Releasing Corporation.
Executive producers: Selig J. Seligman and Peter Zoref.
Produced by Robert Haggiag.
Directed by Christian Marquand.
Screenplay by Buck Henry, based on the novel by Terry Southern and Mason Hoffenberg.
Photographed in Technicolor by Giuseppe Rotunno.
Art director: Dean Tavoularis.
Edited by Giancarlo Cappelli.
Musical score by Dave Grusin.
Running time: 123 minutes.

CAST:

Candy	Ewa Aulin
The Hunchback	Charles Aznavour
Grindl	Marlon Brando
McPhisto	Richard Burton
Dr. Krankeit	James Coburn
Dr. Dunlap	John Huston
General Smight	Walter Matthau
Emmanuel	Ringo Starr
Daddy and Uncle Jack	John Astin
Livia	Elsa Martinelli
Zero	Sugar Ray Robinson
Nurse Bullock	Anita Pallenberg
Silvia	Lea Padovani
Lolita	Florinda Bolkan
Conchita	Marilu Tolo
Marquita	Nicoletta Machiavelli

and members of The Living Theatre

The Terry Southern–Mason Hoffenberg sex-

CANDY

(1968)

spoof novel *Candy* had been available to film producers for almost ten years before it made the transition to the screen. The French actor-director Christian Marquand became obsessed with the idea of making the film but he was unable to persuade any of the major studios to take on the property, the consensus being that the material was too explicit to film for a wide audience. Marquand, who had previously directed only one film, *Le Grand Chemin*, a total flop, received his first sign of a breakthrough when Marlon Brando expressed his enthusiasm for the idea and his willingness to appear in the film. Brando then sold Richard Burton on being involved, and with two major stars on his side Marquand was able to enlist the support of Hollywood producer Selig J. Seligman and Selmur Pictures, a subsidiary of the American Broadcasting Company. The ball began to roll and Marquand and his producer Robert Haggiag soon had a raft of stars eager to play in their picture. Buck Henry was hired to write the screenplay and permitted to build up the original story with extra characters and lavish situations. When an apparent abundance of financial backing the slim novel grew into a huge film, its makers obviously believing that they were involved in a sex comedy that would make a fortune.

As a film *Candy* is a major disaster. It is a monstrous, vulgar vaudeville act as devoid of humor as it is of eroticism. The film assails its audience for two hours with a formless string of eipsodes, illogically linked, in which the young girl of the title is seduced by a series of weird and frantic men, among them: McPhisto (Richard Burton), a flamboyant, drunken Welsh poet lecturer; a super-patriot, bigoted Brigadier General (Walter Matthau); Jonathan J. John (Enrico Maria Salerno), an Andy Warhol-type film maker; a criminal hunchback (Charles Aznavour); a celebrated brain surgeon, frighteningly manic (James Coburn); a Mexican gardener set on priesthood (Ringo Starr); her father and her uncle (John Astin in a dual role); and a guru named Grindl (Brando), who roams the country in a mobile sanctum. Rounding out the frenzied picture are brutal policemen, lesbians, caricatured homosexuals and lascivious spectators.

Marlon Brando comes off better than most of the actors. His is an isolated vignette but it comes toward the end of the film, by which time the audience is insensate. His Grindl, with a precise Indian accent, confuses the none-too-bright Candy with philosophical double-talk, and exhausts himself with his elaborate and lengthy seduction. He elects to teach her the six stages of the mystic path, all of them seemingly sexual, but he collapses before reaching the seventh stage. Brando milks whatever humor he can from the character but his scene, like all the others, is swamped with pretentious photographic effects and a blaring rock-and-roll musical score by Dave Grusin.

Whether the novel could ever have been made into an acceptable film is debatable. Perhaps with a cast of unknown actors and a small budget, one that would not have allowed for excesses, *Candy* might have been an amusing and pleasingly bawdy picture. But in the hands of Christian Marquand it is a wild, juvenile, exhaustingly psychedelic romp in which a number of famous actors have been compromised into appearing offensive and foolish.

With Ewa Aulin

200

With Ewa Aulin

A Gina Production released by Universal Pictures.
Executive Producers: Jerry Gershwin and Elliott Kastner.
Produced and directed by Hubert Cornfield.
Screenplay by Hubert Cornfield and Robert Phippeny, based on the novel *The Snatchers* by Lionel White.
Photographed in Technicolor by Willi Kurout.
Art direction by Jean Boulet.
Edited by Gordon Pilkington.
Musical score by Stanley Myers.
Running time: 93 minutes.

CAST:

Bud (The Chauffeur)	Marlon Brando
Leer	Richard Boone
Blonde	Rita Moreno
Girl	Pamela Franklin
Friendly	Jess Hahn
Gendarme/Fisherman	Gerard Buhr
Bartender	Jacques Marin
The Father	Hughes Wanner
Pilot	All Lettier

The least successful of Marlon Brando's films have been those he has made for Universal. The association between the actor and the studio has been strangely unyielding; *The Ugly American* and *Bedtime Story* both did fair business at the box office but *The Countess from Hong Kong* and *The Appaloosa* can only be described in show business terms as bombs. Sadly *The Night of the Following Day* continues the negative curve. Designed as an off-beat and stylish crime caper it fails to convince either with its plot or its characters. The fault must be laid at the feet of Hubert Cornfield, who not only directed and produced the film but was partly responsible for the script, thereby taking on more than he was capable of handling. The source material was the

THE NIGHT OF THE FOLLOWING DAY

(1969)

novel *The Snatchers* by Lionel White, an expert crime writer whose *The Killing* provided Stanley Kubrick with the basis for a brilliant minor film. Dealing as it does with a kidnapping, a subject that has rarely made for enjoyable or successful films, the odds were against *The Snatchers* being transferred to the screen because such a picture needs to linger on the distasteful and disparate characters of the team of kidnappers. The audience has no choice but to spend time with these unpleasant people and in so doing it becomes obvious that they could never work together as a team and that their scheme is doomed to fail.

The team consists of Brando as a semidecent, enigmatic criminal referred to only as Bud—somewhat ironic since that was Brando's own family nickname—Richard Boone as a sadistic and perverted gentleman appropriately named Leer, and Rita Moreno and Jess Hahn as a brother and sister, the one a drug addict and the other a large, thick-headed thug. The story unfolds with an air liner landing at Paris' Orly Airport. A stewardess (Moreno) is attentive to a teen-age girl (Pamela Franklin) and makes sure her seatbelt is fastened. The girl is met by a uniformed chauffeur (Brando) who drives her away in a limousine. On a country road the limousine comes to a stop and a well-dressed man (Boone) emerges from another car and gets into the limousine. The girl is scared but he quietly tells her not to worry. The limousine stops again at another point and Lear and the girl and the baggage are transferred to a car driven by the airline stewardess. The girl now has reason to assume she is the victim of a plot. The party drives to a lonely cottage on a remote sandy beach. Leer tells the girl, "We are professional criminals."

Contact is arranged with the girl's wealthy father (Hughes Wanner) who is allowed to talk to his daughter on the telephone, after Leer has de-vised a method by which the call cannot be traced. A local fisherman wanders by the cottage and talks to Vi, who nervously explains that she has rented the cottage in order to care for her sick husband. On entering the cottage Vi takes a narcotic to bolster her nerves. Later the same evening, Bud and Vi's brother Wally wait in vain to be picked up by Vi at the local airport. The fisherman, who is also a policeman (Gerard Buhr), gives them a lift to the cottage, assuming them to be medical men. Inside the cottage Bud finds Vi semi-conscious in the bathtub; she tells him that she has taken a sleeping pill but he senses she is back on drugs.

The girl makes an attempt to escape. She manages to get the key to her room and sneaks downstairs. As she walks by Leer, dozing on the staircase, he grabs her leg and starts to beat her. Her screams arouse Bud, who pulls Leer away from the terrified girl and warns him, "If you want to get freaky, don't do it with her." The next day Bud confides in Wally that they should call the whole thing off because the risks are too great, what with a policeman knowing their location, Vi on drugs and Leer a psychopath. Wally fails to see the danger, especially as the whole caper is timed to be over in the next twelve hours. Another complication arises with Vi becoming hysterically jealous of the girl when she sees Bud being solicitous. To stop Vi leaving Bud agrees with the other men that he must pay her sympathetic and amorous attention. Vi takes Leer to the nearby airport, then goes to a local café for a drink. The fisherman-policeman enters and passes time with her. Later as she is driving to the cottage in the rain, she stops to fix her stuck windshield wipers and he appears again. Vi is sure he knows the truth. This may not be the case but it nevertheless plays upon the taut nerves of Vi—and helps give the film a sense of suspense.

With Richard Boone and Pamela Franklin

With Richard Boone, Pamela Franklin and Rita Moreno

With Rita Moreno

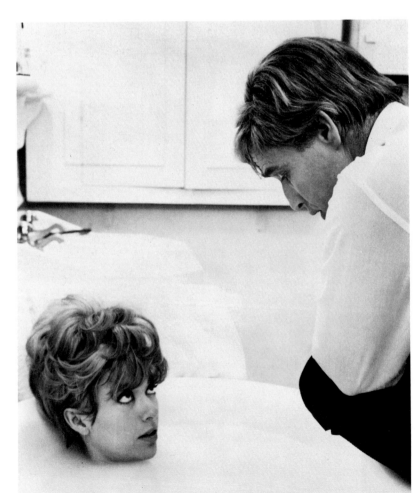

With Rita Moreno

206

With Rita Moreno and Jess Hahn

he will beat the girl and, "you won't want to see the result." Bud joins Vi after placing a time bomb as a diversionary explosion. At the cafe the plans start to go awry when the proprietor locates a gun and wounds Wally. Bud then kills the proprietor and when the fisherman-policeman arrives on the scene he is shot by Vi. They grab the money from the father and race to the cottage. Just prior to their arrival we see Leer, smartly dressed and pulling on his gloves as he says to the girl whom he has ravaged, "Thank you, my dear, for a charming interlude."

With Jess Hahn

In Paris, Leer makes arrangements with the girl's father, who agrees to the ransom. Leer observes the father from a distance as he picks up the money and carries out the instructions. When the father arrives at the local airport Vi is waiting and watching for him. By telephone she instructs him to proceed to the café, where she and her brother will meet him. At the cottage the girl embraces Bud and begs not to be left alone with Leer, but Leer pulls a gun and commands Bud to proceed to the cafe, threatening, "If you're not back in an hour . . ." elaborating that

207

With Hughes Wanner

The final scenes show Leer machine-gunning the car containing his three companions in crime. He kills the brother and sister but Bud manages to escape unharmed. He stalks and shoots Leer as the immaculate man makes his way across the sand, carrying the case of money, and happily striding in his topcoat, homburg and cane. Dying with a smile on his face Leer taunts Bud, "Hey, Lochinvar, what'cha gonna do now." Bud then enters the cottage and finds the girl, hanging by her hands, stripped to the waist and bleeding from cuts. Gently he cuts her down and as the dazed girl comes to her senses she finds herself sitting in an airplane being awakened by a stewardess. It's all been a dream!

Few critics greeted *The Night of the Following Day* with anything other than derision. It found no favor with the public and Universal released it to television two years later, after deftly editing out a few profane words and several moments of sexual sadism. Most critics lambasted the script, not only for its improbable plotting and its du-

bious and despicable characters but for its dialogue. Brando's Bud, a character he obviously saw as deeper than as written, is none too articulate, speaking in a shallow kind of jive talk and ending every other utterance with "man." But as with every Brando film it is his mere presence and his strangely mesmeric acting that holds the attention of the viewer. Richard Boone is a similarly charismatic actor with a genius for playing dangerous men of rough, frightening charm. Rita Moreno was excellent as the distraught female accomplice, and in judging the performance of Pamela Franklin sympathy must be brought to bear. It is a distasteful role and the young English actress might well have been actually terrified in playing her brutal sex scenes with Boone. Greatly in the film's favor are the locations—Paris and particularly the seascapes of the northern coast of France, subtly color photographed by Willi Kurout. For Brando it was another interesting failure, unfortunately so in view of its long line of similarly categorizable predecessors.

With Jacques Marin

An Alberto Grimaldi Production, co-produced with Produzioni Europee Associates (Rome) and Les Productions Artistes Associes (Paris). Released by United Artists.
Produced by Alberto Grimaldi.
Directed by Gillo Pontecorvo.
Screenplay by Franco Solinas and Giorgio Arlorio, based on an original story by Gillo Pontecorvo, Franco Solinas and Giorgio Arlorio.
Photographed in Deluxe Color by Marcello Gatti.
Art direction by Sergio Canevari.
Edited by Mario Morra.
Musical score by Ennio Morricone.
Running time: 112 minutes.

CAST:

Sir William Walker	Marlon Brando
José Dolores	Evaristo Marquez
Teddy Sanchez	Renato Salvatori
Shelton	Norman Hill
General Prada	Tom Lyons
Guarina	Wanani
Juanito	Joseph Persuad
Henry	Gianpiero Albertini
Jack	Carlo Pammucci
Lady Bella	Cecily Browne
Francesca	Dana Ghia
Ramon	Maurice Rodriguez
English Major	Alejandro Obregon

Marlon Brando's involvement in the making of *Burn!* came about directly as the result of his political idealism and his desire to make films with a comment on the human situation. In 1968 he was deeply involved in supporting civil rights causes, particularly those pertaining to black and Indian conditions, and, according to his friends, he was greatly disturbed and depressed by the

210

BURN!

(1970)

assassinations of Robert Kennedy and Martin Luther King. Brando was ripe for a film that might express his sense of outrage. He had admired Gillo Pontecorvo's brilliant picture *The Battle of Algiers*, which won an Oscar nomination as the best foreign film of 1967, and told the director he would be interested in working with him. Pontecorvo's *The Battle of Algiers* is a keenly political film and it has served as a kind of rallying cry for the youth of the western world. *Burn!* is an indictment of colonialism, international Big Business, and slavery, and at the outset Pontecorvo claimed it as an intention to "join the romantic adventure and the film of ideas." In Brando he found a fervent ally but unfortunately the actor and director also found that once they began working together their views on dramatic interpretations were not in accord, and by the end of the difficult nine months of production they were not on speaking terms. Brando maintains his admiration for Pontecorvo's talent but looking back on the labors of this film he says, "I could have killed him."

Trouble began to brew for the production even before it started. The story, which Pontecorvo put together with Franco Solinas (the scenarist on all the director's previous pictures) and Giorgio Arlorio, takes as its inspiration the historical fact that in 1520 the Spaniards razed a Caribbean island in order to quell a native uprising. The island was thereafter known as Quemada, the Spanish word for burnt. The Spaniards replaced the exterminated population with a colony of Negro slaves and set up the island as a sugar-cane industry, with the proceeds sent to Spain for the next three centuries. The present-day Spanish government made known their objections to the film, refusing the company permission to film any sequences in Spain, and threatening to boycott it in any part of the world

in which they had influence. The Italian and French producers then decided to shift the onus to the Portuguese; the original title of the film was to have been *Quemada*, but now the letter *i* was added to give it the Portuguese spelling of *Queimada*, and it was released with that title in most parts of the world. In North America its distributors, United Artists, took a dim view of the film's commercial possibilities and decided to translate the title. Their gloomy predictions proved true and this odd but interesting picture is listed in their books as a loser.

Burn! begins in 1845 as Sir William Walker (Brando) arrives on the island of Queimada, seemingly an innocent traveler but actually an agent of the British government, instructed to instigate a revolution that will break the Portuguese hold on the island and allow the British to take control of the valuable sugar-cane output. Queimada has a population of two hundred thousand, of whom only five thousand are Europeans. The main town is a well-protected port with a fort and a garrison, a governor's palace, a cathedral, a bank, a hotel and a brothel. The chess-playing English gentleman realizes he must play the part of a political Pygmalion. He looks around for a likely subject to train as a revolutionary and he picks upon José Dolores (Evaristo Marquez), a large, handsome black dock-worker with an air of confidence. Walker also enlists Teddy Sanchez (Renato Salvatori), an almost-white clerk with political ambitions. Walker persuades José Dolores to rob the bank of a large amount of gold bullion, and once he does so Walker reveals the robber to the government, thereby turning Dolores into a hunted outlaw. The cunning Walker then instructs Dolores and his followers in the use of firearms and instills in them the idea of overthrowing the Portuguese government on the island.

211

With Evaristo Marquez

With Renato Salvatori

Walker makes his next move on the annual, festival day of Negro freedom. Once a year the slaves are allowed to swarm through the streets in costume, singing and dancing. A group of hooded men make their way into the governor's palace, led by Walker and Sanchez, and it is Walker's hand which steadies the aim of Sanchez as he fires at the governor and kills him. And it is Walker who pushes Sanchez out on the balcony to receive the cheers of the mob, who greet him as the hero of the revolution. Walker's scheme has succeeded—the economic policy which bound the island to Portugal has been broken and it is open to the world market. José Dolores, an inspiring rebel leader but a man incapable of government, agrees to disband his army and allow Teddy Sanchez to assume the presidency. Sanchez signs an agreement with England, giving that country major control of the island's sugar-cane output, and Walker returns to London.

Ten years pass. Walker becomes a drunken drifter but because of his previous accomplishments in Queimada the British sugar merchants employ him to return to the island, where trouble has arisen with corruption in the Sanchez regime and another revolution led by José Dolores.

British interests are now at stake and Walker recognizes the need to eliminate his pupil. Fields, forests and villages are burned in the warfare between Dolores' guerrilla bands and the British military units directed by Walker, and Sanchez comes to the realization that his country is being used by the British. Before he can do much damage with this realization Walker has the president arrested and shot by a firing squad for high treason. Then, adding Sanchez' own black troops to the British forces, Walker eventually wins the fight against José Dolores, but only after much of the island has been ruined by fire and pillage. The tutor and the subdued pupil come face to face: Sir William tells José, "It was inevitable that you had to lose." José refuses to accept Walker's outstretched hand, and he also refuses to take advantage of Walker's offer of escape, preferring to be executed and become a martyr to his people. The confused Walker asks him, "What kind of revenge is it if you're dead?" and Jose replies, "If a man gives you freedom, it is not freedom. Freedom is something you take for yourself." The implication is that history will be on his side, not Walker's.

Walker has defeated himself by creating a true

214

With Renato Salvatori

revolutionary. With the island's troubled quelled, Walker prepares to leave. He makes his way through the crowds to his boat and—in a scene reminiscent of his first meeting with José Dolores —a black man offers to carry his suitcases. Walker hands them over but the hand that moves toward him carries a knife. The blade flashes through the air and the Englishman falls dead.

The best moments in *Burn!* are Pontecorvo's handling of his action sequences and his deft manipulating of large numbers of extras—almost twenty thousand were used in Colombia. This same talent is vividly apparent in his *The Battle of Algiers,* in which he staged exciting, violent street fights that looked as if they might actually have been newsreel footage. In *Burn!* Pontecorvo directed brilliant episodes involving large numbers of Colombians, such as the wild carnival that acts as a cover for the assassination of the governor, the victorious black soldiers running and galloping along the beaches, the riots in the villages, and the battles in the mountains that culminate in the capture of José Dolores. The film is much less effective in its acting and its long winded story-telling. *Burn!* runs 132 min-

utes as edited by Mario Morra, but twenty minutes have been lopped off the prints available in the United States and Canada, making it difficult to pass an opinion on the film as finished by Pontecorvo. But even at 112 minutes, it is still long and wavering.

Burn! is quite obviously political in tone, perhaps a little too simplistically Marxist, but it is a passionate piece of propaganda in the anti-colonial struggle. Parallels with Vietnam may be inferred and in this instance some American critics pointed out that it was refreshing to find Great Britain the villain, rather than the United States. Pontecorvo gave himself enormous problems by deciding to shoot his film in Colombia, making his headquarters in Cartagena, involving transporting a huge crew and masses of equipment to a remote location. The film took a full nine months to shoot and on the final day Pontecorvo had only ten of his original crew members with him. Most of the footage was shot in Colombia but Marlon Brando tired of the long stay in the dull area and after many arguments with the director over concepts and methods of filming, he left and told Pontecorvo the film would have to be finished elsewhere. The sequence involving the capture of José Dolores ended up being shot in the mountains near Marrakech, Morocco; the London sequences were shot in the Cinecitta Studios in Rome; the scene of a brigantine approaching the port of Queimada was filmed in St. Thomas, Virgin Islands; and the port activity was staged in San Malo, in northern France. No figures have been released by the producers of this French-Italian co-production as to its final cost, or to its income. But it may safely be assumed that returns from its showings in North America will account for only a portion of its earnings.

Marlon Brando's interpretation of Sir William Walker is reminiscent of his Fletcher Christian. This is another rather foppish English gentleman, whose gentle speech and soft manners mask an iron will and tough intentions. Walker, as understood by Brando, is not a villain but merely a pragmatist with a difficult job to do. The differences between the actor and the director arose over the concept of Walker; the intense and thoroughly sincere Pontecorvo saw him as the evil catalyst of the story but Brando wanted to play him in a humanistic light, with a bemused manner and an outrageous sense of humor. *Burn!* suffers from being a heavy-handed film and Brando gives it its only lightness. Pontecorvo, who had directed only three films prior to this, added to his burdens by insisting on a largely amateur cast. Half of the principal players had never acted before, and as Brando's co-star Pontecorvo selected Evaristo Marquez, an illiterate Colombian cane-cutter who not only had never acted but who had never even seen a film. Brando coached Marquez but much time was wasted getting a performance out of him, sometimes calling for dozens of takes on a scene. Language was another problem; Brando spoke to his director in French, to the crew in Italian and to his fellow actors in Spanish.

Sadly, what can be said about *Burn!* can also be said about the dozen Brando pictures which preceded it: interesting but disappointing, particularly for the investors. At this point in his career Marlon Brando was a star badly in need of an upward turning point.

With Evaristo Marquez

With Evaristo Marquez

219

With Stephanie Beacham

An Elliott Kastner–Jay Kanter–Alan Ladd, Jr.–Scimitar production released by Avco Embassy.
Produced and directed by Michael Winner.
Screenplay by Michael Hastings, based on characters from *The Turn of the Screw*, by Henry James.
Photographed in Technicolor by Robert Paynter.
Art direction by Herbert Westbrook.
Edited by Frederick Wilson.
Musical score by Jerry Fielding.
Running time: 96 minutes.

CAST:

Peter Quint	Marlon Brando
Margaret Jessel	Stephanie Beacham
Mrs. Grose	Thora Hird
Flora	Verna Harvey
Miles	Christopher Ellis
Master of the House	Harry Andrews
Governess	Anna Palk

It is not uncommon in the film business for scenarists to develop sequels to famous stories but it is rare to find a screenplay that is an entire supposition of situations preceding a famous tale. Such is Michael Hastings' *The Nightcomers*, a 96-minute overture to Henry James' celebrated novel *The Turn of the Screw*, stylishly directed and produced by Michael Winner as a low-keyed, genteel horror picture. The idea is intriguing because the two ghosts of the James original become the two main characters of the film and Hastings has invented a fairly credible account of how and why the characters die, and why they should haunt and corrupt the children in *The Turn of the Screw*. In the novel Peter Quint and Margaret Jessel are already dead, due to circumstances never explained by James. As ghosts they return to claim the souls of two children, Miles

THE NIGHTCOMERS

(1972)

and Flora, in Bly House, an affluent country estate in England at the turn of the century. Their governess struggles to save the children from the malevolent spirits. William Archibald dramatized the novel and it appeared as a stage play, "The Innocents," in 1950. Composer Benjamin Britten and lyricist Myfanwy Piper made the novel into an opera in 1954, using the original title, and a few years later the play was done on television with Ingrid Bergman as the governess. In 1961, Truman Capote assisted playwright Archibald in adapting his work into a screenplay and it was filmed in England with Deborah Kerr in the role of the governess. Hastings and Winner therefore needed a fair measure of courage in tackling a preamble to so well-established a story. They also had the inspired idea of offering the role of Peter Quint to Marlon Brando, thereby giving the actor his first really colorful part in a long time.

The Nightcomers begin in somewhat the same manner as *The Turn of the Screw* by establishing the fact that the wealthy gentleman who is the Master of Bly House (Harry Andrews) has fallen heir to a pair of children and cannot be bothered to act as their guardian. He turns them over to his housekeeper and a governess and leaves Bly House to live at his home in London. The children, 12-year-old Miles and his one-year-older sister Flora, have lost their parents in an automobile accident. Neither the housekeeper, Mrs. Grose (Thora Hird), or the governess, Miss Jessel (Stephanie Beacham), see fit to tell the children about the loss of their parents, and the news is broken to them by Quint, an Irishman of blarney and calculated charm, who is the master's valet until the master leaves Bly House, and he is then demoted to handyman and gardener. Quint captivates the children with his roughhewn philosophy, his crude anecdotes about his background and his willingness to play with them. He grad-

ually becomes their mentor and his views on life and death permeate their thinking.

It is Quint's attitude toward death that seals his own fate, and that of Miss Jessel. On one occasion as he plays with the children in the country he lights a cigar and places it in the mouth of a toad. As the toad inhales it swells up and, unable to exhale, it eventually explodes. The children are horrified but Quint explains that the toad was in a state of ecstasy and died happy. With irresponsible aplomb he persuades them that love and hate are much the same thing, that it possible to want to kill someone you love, and that the dead go nowhere, they simply stay where they are. Being at a highly impressionable age, and isolated from life, these thoughts insidiously warp the minds of the children.

Quint does them further damage inadvertently. Miles follows him at night as he creeps into the house and proceeds to the room of the prim and proper Miss Jessel. The frightened young woman silently subjects herself to his rough sexual molesting. He strips her and ties her hands and feet to the bedposts before beating her and making love to her. All of this is observed by the spying boy, who later relates the experience to his sister and forces her to submit to similar treatment. They are discovered by the horrified Mrs. Grose, who demands to know what the children are doing, to which Miles cheerfully admits, "We are doing sex." The housekeeper brings this to the attention of Miss Jessel, who has already found the children difficult to deal with. She is, in fact, only the latest in a line of governesses. Miss Jessel, at first repelled by the insolent Quint, now realizes she, in her loneliness and her awakened sexuality, is also drawn to the man.

Miss Jessel's dilemma deepends when the housekeeper begins to suspect her affair with

221

With Stephanie Beacham

Quint. Mrs. Grose observes the bruises on the face of the governess and receives only evasive explanations. One night Mrs. Grose steals into Miss Jessel's room, thinking Quint might be there. He isn't, but the governess pulls back the covers on her nude body to welcome her sado-masochistic lover and finds her visitor is not the one she expected. Mrs. Grose, quite class-conscious and ever at odds with Quint, now has ample reason to fire both him and the governess. But she reckons without the machinations of the cunning children, now very perverse in their views of life. Without deliberately doing so, Quint has corrupted them and his mysterious thoughts are twisted to suit their own reasoning.

The children seize upon a plan to keep Quint

With Verna Harvey and Christopher Ellis

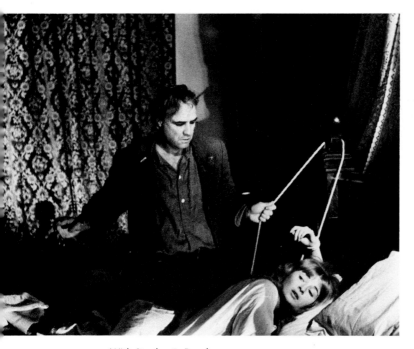

With Stephanie Beacham

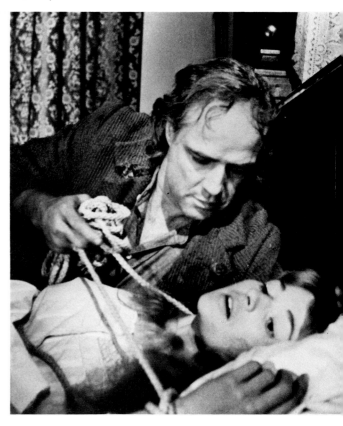

With Stephanie Beacham

With Verna Harvey

With Christopher Ellis

225

With Verna Harvey

With Thora Hird

With Stephanie Beacham

With Stephanie Beacham

226

and Miss Jessel from leaving. They convince the governess that Quint is waiting for her at a little summer house on an island in a lake. Unable to swim and terrified of water she makes her uneasy way across the lake in a row-boat, but the children have smashed a hole in the bottom and it sinks, leaving Miss Jessel to die a horrible death in the water. The next day Quint walks near the lake and spots the half-submerged body lying in the mud. He wades in and pulls it to shore, looking with amazement at the stiff, macabre corpse. As he proceeds toward the house he is stopped by Miles; the boy is carrying a long-bow, with a quiver of arrows on his back—Quint having previously taught the boy to shoot. As Quint sits on a log, gazing at the ground and trying to think what to do, Miles shoots an arrow into his head. Quint tries to get up, staggers a few pace and sinks to his knees. Miles smiles as he tells him, "It won't be long now, Quint," and he shoots another arrow into his head. Quint slumps into a puddle. Miles and Flora, pleased with themselves, believe that they have united the lovers, and since "the dead stay where they are" Quint and Miss Jessel will remain with them. Later, when Mrs. Grose presents a new governess (Anna Palk) to Miles and Flora, the children look at her with a strange smile on their lovely, innocent faces, and as Miles conceals a toad behind his back the audience has every right to think that the post of the governess will not be a comfortable one.

The Nightcomers may not be entirely believable but it is a fascinating speculation, mounted and acted in an expert manner. The film was made entirely on location—Michael Winner refuses to film in studios—in Cambridgeshire and using a genuine, handsome old country manor. Winner wisely set his Gothic tale in the autumn and winter and the bleakness of the simple English countryside lends itself to the chilly character of the screenplay. The producer also decided not to follow the script's original instructions and show the children in explicit sexual acts; as it is they are seen fully clothed and engaging only in the typing-up of Flora. This would have been a shocking and distasteful scene in a film already markedly erotic and horrific. The sex scenes are artfully directed by Winner in a series of dissolves which sensually suggest the gratification of Quint and the titillation of Miles. The photography of Robert Paynter and a delicate, moody and tuneful (sometimes touching on English folk themes) score by Jerry Fielding give the picture an atmospheric sense of muted horror beneath its gentle surface.

Michael Winner, a young Englishman whose wide-ranging interests have produced films as different as *I'll Never Forget What's 'Isname* to *Lawman* looks upon *The Nightcomers* as a film that cannot help but suggest different things to different people: "I suppose to me it says that we are born innocent; we are perverted by what we see. For we all of us look around at the same sights and see different things. We are colored by the life within us viewing the life outside us. Nothing is real because it is only seen in our interpretation. Each person can swear to his own truth, but it is not the truth of anyone else. The young open their eyes to the old, and are assured confusion."

Peter Quint is one of Marlon Brando's most complex performances, and a more interesting one than the several which precede this film. His Quint, with a quiet Irish accent, is devious and disturbed. He is spellbinding in his scenes with the children, telling them of his adventures, and strangely vicious and aberrant in his dealings with the governess. The perverse character is split-levelled, kind and attentive on the one and ruthless and bitter on the other. It is an eloquent performance in which Brando achieves the greatly difficult art of making Quint likable, pitiable and frightening. Only the most accomplished actor could cover such a diverse range in one characterization.

227

An Albert S. Ruddy Production, released by Paramount Pictures.
Produced by Albert S. Ruddy.
Associate Producer: Gary Frederickson.
Directed by Francis Ford Coppola.
Screenplay by Mario Puzo and Francis Ford Coppola, based on the novel by Puzo.
Photographed in Technicolor by Gordon Willis.
Art direction by Warren Clymer.
Edited by William Reynolds and Peter Zinner.
Musical score by Nino Rota.
Running time: 176 minutes.

CAST:

Don Vito Corleone	Marlon Brando
Michael Corleone	Al Pacino
Sonny Corleone	James Caan
Clemenza	Richard Castellano
Tom Hagen	Robert Duvall
McCluskey	Sterling Hayden
Jack Woltz	John Marley
Barzini	Richard Conte
Kay Adams	Diane Keaton
Sollozzo	Al Lettieri
Tessio	Abe Vigoda
Connie Rizzi	Talia Shire
Carlo Rizzi	Gianni Russo
Fredo Corleone	John Cazale
Cuneo	Rudy Bond
Johnny Fontane	Al Martino
Mama Corleone	Morgana King
Luca Brasi	Lenny Montana
Paulie Gatto	John Martino
Bonasera	Salvatore Corsitto
Neri	Richard Bright
Moe Greene	Alex Rocco
Bruno Tattaglia	Tony Giorgio
Nazorine	Vito Scotti
Theresa Hagen	Tere Livrano

THE GODFATHER

(1972)

Phillip Tattaglia	Victor Rendina
Lucy Mancini	Jeannie Linero
Sandra Corleone	Julie Gregg
Mrs. Clemenza	Ardell Sheridan
Apollonia	Simonetta Stefanelli
Fabrizio	Angelo Infanti
Don Tommasino	Corrado Gaipa
Calo	Franco Citti
Vitelli	Saro Urzi

Mario Puzo claims he had Marlon Brando in mind as Don Vito Corleone while he was writing *The Godfather*. He sold the rights to Paramount Pictures before the book was finished and received $35,000, plus an understanding that he would also either write, or collaborate on, the screenplay for a fee of $100,000 and a small percentage on the returns from the film. Paramount was not enthusiastic about *The Godfather* at the outset; they had lost money on *The Brotherhood*, Kirk Douglas's view of the Mafia, and they instructed Puzo to design his screenplay as a contemporary crime story and not a study of a criminal empire. The studio allocated a modest two million dollars as the budget and hired Al Ruddy as producer and Francis Ford Coppola as director, both of them men in their early thirties. Ruddy and Coppola admit that their backgrounds in the film business were not impressive enough to qualify them as the producer and director of *The Godfather* as it finally emerged. Ruddy had been involved in television and a few minor films, and Coppola had directed *You're a Big Boy Now*, *Finian's Rainbow*, and *The Rain People*, none of them winners at the box office. But Coppola was regarded in Hollywood as a film maker with vitality and style, and he was respected as a writer, having won an Oscar as co-scripter of *Patton*.

Ruddy and Coppola persuaded Paramount to invest more money in *The Godfather*, a persuasion that was hard to resist with the sales of Puzo's book spreading like a bush fire through the literary world. These sales were concurrent with the preparation of the picture, and before it was ready for showing to the public, *The Godfather* as a book had sold half a million copies in hardback and something like ten million copies in paperback. As the sales increased so Ruddy and Coppola twisted the corporate arm of Paramount; they dismissed the mild screenplay Puzo had prepared at the instruction of the studio, and Coppola and the author then sat down to write a literal translation of the book. The burning question in the minds of the film industry and the public was—who would play the title role? Ruddy and Coppola wanted either Marlon Brando or Sir Laurence Olivier. The great English actor begged off, explaining that he did not feel well enough to tackle the part, thus leaving the way open for Brando, who read the book in three days after the producer gave it to him and immediately agreed to play the role. When Ruddy and Coppola told this to the upper echelon at Paramount, the studio adamantly refused to consider Brando, complaining that his flops were now too many and that the public was no longer drawn by his name.

For the first time in his film career Marlon Brando agreed to make a screen test, although not the usual kind. Producer Ruddy took a videotape unit to Brando's home in the Hollywood hills and the actor agreed to go along with Ruddy's plan. Says the producer, "Marlon just put some black make-up under his eyes, streaked his hair with grey and pulled it back, pencilled a moustache, and puffed out his cheeks with toilet paper. He just sat there, sipping on a little cup of coffee and puffing one of those Italian cigars—

With Salvatori Corsitto

no talk, just expressions—and there he was, Don Corleone. Paramount flipped when they saw the test; Bob Evans (head of production) said, 'He looks Italian, fine. But who is it? It turned them all around on Marlon.''

Brando's main problem in approaching the part was one of age. He was forty-seven at the time of filming *The Godfather* but the film required him to play a man twenty years his senior, and to age several more years during the course of the story. To help Brando with the physical aspect of his task Ruddy hired Dick Smith, a make-up genius with a specialty for *aging*. Smith prepared Hal Holbrook for the television presentation of *Mark Twain Tonight*, and he made a grizzled old relic of Dustin Hoffman in *Little Big Man*. He is also the creator of latex character masks and facial pieces. Smith explains his solution in aging Brando: "My main objective was to keep the make-up basic and simple. The primary method in aging Brando was wrinkling his skin, which we created by an application of liquid latex around the eyes and wherever else the effect was desired. Wrinkles were formed by combining the liquid latex with the stretching of the natural skin and heavier applications of this material were utilized to give Brando a more leathery appearance as he aged. To produce the sags and loose facial flesh we created a denture consisting of a band of metal designed to fit around

Brando's lower teeth and change his bite. A gum-like substance was then inserted at the jaw line to produce simulated jowls. He dyed his hair to black-brown and added gray tones. In other respects making him up was a matter of color detail such as increasing the aging look with the application of 'paintbox' liver spots and tiny wrinkles. We also used olive skin tones as well as dark eye make-up in order to create a more Mediterranean look. The rest was up to Brando.''

The "rest" that was up to Brando proved to be one of the most arresting performances ever given by an actor in films. His Don Corleone is a tough old Sicilian peasant who has risen to become an omnipotent chieftain in an empire of Italian-American crime. He is the leader of one of the five families who are said to control the Mafia in the area of New York. He is indeed a family man, in the exact sense of the word—his sons and his relatives are part of his operation and he expects, and receives, total loyalty and devotion. Perhaps the most fascinating contradiction of *The Godfather* is that although it is a story of crime, replete with much violence and brutal killings, it is also a story of a family adhering to their own moral codes, the strongest of which is their concern for each other. The Corleones are a warm, close family and this film shows the flavor of Italian-American home life. Don Corleone is an undisputed patriarch, and as

With Robert Duvall, Tere Livrano, John Cazale, Gianni Russo, Talia Shire, Morgana King, James Caan and Julia Gregg

With Al Pacino, James Caan and John Cazale

played by Brando he has almost the manner of a religious leader. His voice is quiet and rasping, his chin sticks out as a symbol of his authority, and men kiss his hand as they seek his favors. There is a remoteness about him, and his watchful old eyes reflect his benevolence and his implacability.

The opening shot of *The Godfather* sets the tone of the film: the color photography is muted and dim as Don Corleone and some of his family listen as an undertaker, Bonasera (Salvatore Cirsitto), asks for help. His daughter has been brutally raped by two men, non-Italians, who have been pardoned by a judge. Bonasera pleads for justice. The Don listens without a trace of emotion, as he strokes a cat, and he reminds Bonasera that the undertaker has previously shown him no respect or interest. But Bonasera is touching in his anguish and the Don promises him that the two men will be "dealt with," and that the undertaker may one day be called to return the favor. The Don and his sons then go about the real business of the day—attending the marriage of his daughter Connie (Talia Shire) to young bookmaker Carlo Rizzi (Gianni Russo). The Corleone mansion and the gardens are full

of hundreds of guests, enjoying a lavish banquet and dancing to an Italian band. The time is August of 1945 and the Don's youngest son, Michael (Al Pacino) has just arrived home from the war, still wearing the decorated uniform of a marine captain. Michael is college-educated and it is the hope of his father that the boy will rise to legitimate prominence in politics. With Michael is his non-Italian girlfriend Kay (Diane Keaton).

The marriage party is further enlivened by the arrival of the greatly popular crooner, Johnny Fontane (Al Martino), who sings a love song for the newlyweds and draws the adulation of the young girls in the crowd. His mood changes when he talks to Don Corleone in the house. Fontane, too, has a favor to ask; he wants an important part in a Hollywood film, a job he feels will lift his career, but the producer has refused it to him. The Don sends his right-hand man, legal adviser and adopted son, Tom Hagen (Robert Duvall), to negotiate with producer Jack Woltz (John Marley), who still refuses to consider Fontane. The next morning the producer wakes up to find the severed head of his favorite horse in his bed. Fontane gets the film.

234

With Talia Shire

Back in New York Hagen arranges a meeting between Don Corleone and Virgil Sollozzo (Al Lettieri) of the Tattaglia family, close rivals of the Corleones. Sollozzo proposes that the Don consider joining him in a new and promising avenue of crime, the wide circulation of narcotics in America. Don Corleone flatly refuses to partake of a crime he believes to be not only evil but dangerous in the extreme. However, his son, Sonny (James Caan), is not as morally scrupulous as his father and Sollozzo senses this. A few weeks later Don Corleone is gunned down in the streets, clearly as a way of eliminating him in order to do business with his unsuspecting son. The old man survives and when he recovers, Michael, previously uninvolved with crime, decides to follow the family trade. He agrees to meet Sollozzo and a crooked police captain, McClusky (Sterling Hayden), and instead of making a deal with them, he kills the pair. To remove him from any possible reaction to the killings, the family sends him to Sicily, where he lives for two years and marries a local girl, Appollonia (Simonetta Stefanelli). The idyll is ended by the slaughter of his wife in a car explosion, a reprisal engineered by one of his own bodyguards. Michael returns to New York, now fully intent on an active career in the underworld.

The rival families jockey for the control of the lucrative criminal enterprises of New York and its environs. The aging Don meets with his rivals and states his position on cooperation and unity. They agree with him and seemingly arrive at an understanding, but it is a false front and they continue to manipulate their *industry* to their own ends. Sonny is trapped and shot to death, leaving Michael with the realization that he must assume command of his family. He marries his previous girlfriend, Kay, and settles down to a life much like that of his father. Don Corleone, playing with a grandson in the garden, is stricken with a heart attack and dies.

Michael Corleone becomes the new Godfather and soon shows signs of being tougher and more ruthless than the departed Don, although maintaining family loyalty and every aspect of a respectable businessman. With military precision he arranges the complete elimination of all his enemies, all the rivals who have harmed his family, all his opposition. *The Godfather* ends with a fantastic montage of multiple slaughter, cutting back and forth from a baptism service in a

With Robert Duvall

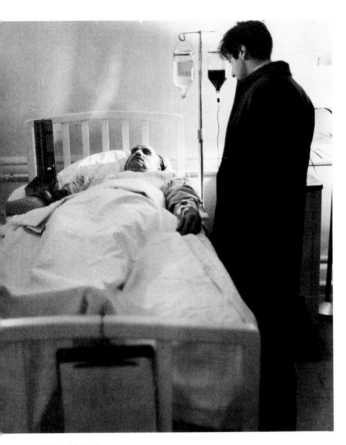

With Al Pacino

church attended by Michael, and the various locations in which his men kill his rivals. The murders restore the Corleones to supreme leadership in the underworld, with the gentle, dignified Michael now the most powerful chieftain in American crime.

The Godfather is a massive piece of film entertainment, three hours of intricate storytelling involving sentiment, nostalgia, filial affection, and epic bloodletting. Within weeks of its release it was clearly a blockbuster that would inevitably take its place among the handful of most profitable films ever made. Wherever it was shown people flocked to see it, and it covered its six million dollar cost in a matter of months. The critics were uniform in praising the film for its magnificent composition, its almost flawless acting and its brilliant direction but most of them added a rueful note about its moral implications. How could they, the critics, and the public be so entertained by a film about the politics of organized crime? Those involved in the making of the picture hasten to explain that it is not a documentary, not a condonation of the Mafia, but a fictional story about people in a certain section of society. Those who made *The Godfather* did

With Abe Vigoda, John Cazale, Al Lettieri and Robert Duvall

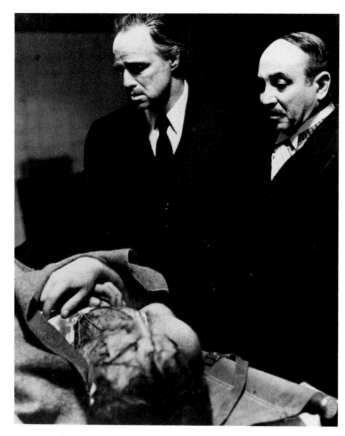

With James Caan and Salvatori Corsitto

Brando embraces Victor Rendina as Richard Conte applauds

their jobs stunningly well, with the result that the film has become a phenomenon—a curious mixture of fantasy and disguised facts, made even more bizarre by the well-publicized facts that dozens of hoodlums died in internecine warfare in New York even as the film was being made in that city. The picture tends to support the familiar cry from the underworld, "We only kill each other," which regrettably happens to be far from the truth.

The fact that the Mafia and the Cosa Nostra seem to enjoy *The Godfather* as much as the general public has the sociologists even more concerned about the moral impact of the film. Initially it was the Italian-American groups in New York who were most opposed to the film being made, and various members of the underworld made known to Paramount that if the company expected to be able to shoot the film in New York, they would make it impossible unless the words "Mafia" and "Cosa Nostra" were not used in the screenplay. The Italian-American Civil Rights League staged a rally in Madison Square Garden and raised $600,000 for the purpose of stopping the film. It is interesting to note that Frank Sinatra was a member of that movement, and that the role of Johnny Fontane is widely believed to be patterned on his career. Says producer Al Ruddy, "We had to get the word out to the Italian-American community in a very bona fide way that we had no intention of doing a schlock exploitation gangster film." Ruddy met with several prominent citizens and convinced them of his purpose, and in making the picture he received very little hindrance and considerable help.

Actual production on *The Godfather* began in New York on March 29, 1971, with Marlon Brando's involvement being limited to a 35-day shooting period between April 12 and May 28, in order to free him for his next commitment. This arrangement worked out as planned, and Brando behaved in a friendly, cooperative manner that left the director and the actors wondering how he could have acquired a reputation for being difficult. The major difficulty shooting the film on location was the period setting of the story, requiring the use of clothes and automobiles of the postwar years. Television antennas had to be removed and all billboards and movie marquees had to pertain to the period. The hardest scenes to shoot were those on Mott Street, a narrow road left over from the horse-and-buggy era, bordering between Little Italy and Chinatown. Spectators jammed the windows and the fire escapes to watch Brando being gunned down in the street, and it took three days to film the sequence. Dozens of other locations were used in Manhattan, the Bronx, Brooklyn and Richmond, where a quiet side street in a residential area of Staten Island was used as the Corleone Family Mall. The location was secluded but it was further isolated by building an eight-foot wall around the garden of the house that was leased as the home of the family. The interiors of the home were shot at the Filmways Studio in the Bronx, and the producers secured permission to film scenes in Bellevue Hospital and the New York Eye and Ear Clinic. In addition to the New York locations, which account for the bulk of the film, the company spent two weeks on location in a small village in Sicily.

Marlon Brando agrees with those who look upon *The Godfather* as a dark comment on certain aspects of American life. He feels that it might even be taken as an allegory on corporate thinking, and that Don Corleone is a somewhat perverse manifestation of the American Dream. He told *Newsweek* reporter Steve Saler, "In a way the Mafia is the best example of capitalists we have. Don Corleone is just an ordinary business magnate who is trying to do the best he can for the group he represents and for his family . . . unlike some corporate heads, Corleone has an unwavering loyalty for the people that have given support to him and his causes and he takes care of his own." Brando went on to say he didn't see much difference between the tactics of the Mafia and the American government, which comments have brought him criticism in some quarters for being too free with his opinions. The *Wall Street Journal* pointed out that there must surely be a difference between the Cosa Nostra and Gulf and Western, who own Paramount, and a difference between machine-gunning or garroting someone, and hiring a detective to trail him.

If *The Godfather* is a glorification of free enterprise gone mad, the film itself is also a glorious piece of evidence that capitalism still works in a legitimate way. By the end of 1972 *The Godfather* has grossed something like one hundred million dollars, and it will continue to earn big money for years to come. Mario Puzo made one and a half million dollars on royalties from his book, and stands to make another two million dollars from his percentage deal on the film. Wonderful though this may seem, it pales when compared with Marlon Brando's luck with *The Godfather*. Brando agreed to take a salary of $100,000, far less than his usual wages for a film, but gambled on taking "a piece of the action." Brando's contract calls for 2½ percent of the first ten million earned by the picture, then 5 percent afterward up to twenty-five million, and after that 20 percent up to one hundred million. Once *The Godfather* touches that figure, Marlon Brando's "piece of the action" represents sixteen million dollars—before taxes.

With Al Pacino

An Alberto Grimaldi Production
Released by United Artists
Produced by Alberto Grimaldi
Directed by Bernardo Bertolucci
Screenplay by Bernardo Bertolucci and Franco Arcalli
Director of photography, Vittorio Storare (A.I.C.)
Cameraman, Enrico Umetelli
Musical score by Gato Barbieri

CAST:

Paul	Marlon Brando
Jeanne	Maria Schneider
Concierge	Darling Legitimus
Tom	Jean-Pierre Leaud
TV script girl	Catherine Sola
TV cameraman	Mauro Marchetti
TV sound engineer	Dan Diament
TV assistant cameraman	Peter Schommer
Catherine	Catherine Allegret
Monique	Marie-Helene Breillat
Mouchette	Catherine Breillat
Rosa's mother	Maria Michi
Rosa	Veronica Lazare
Marcel	Massimo Girotti
President of tango jury	Mimi Pinson

Last Tango in Paris was shot in Paris in February, March and April of 1972 and then went into a long period of editing, due to a great amount of footage, much of it of an improvisatory nature. Expectations were high even before the filming began, partly because of the involvement of Marlon Brando, now expected to take advantage of the renewed interest in his career brought on by *The Godfather*, and partly because the film is the

LAST TANGO IN PARIS

(1972)

creation of the brilliant, 31-year-old Bernardo Bertolucci. Bertolucci had made five films prior to this—*The Grim Reaper, Before the Revolution, Partner, The Spider's Strategy,* and *The Conformist,* the last bringing him an award from the American National Society of Film Critics as the best director of 1971. All the Bertolucci films have been exhibited at major film festivals, with considerable approval.

Produced by Alberto Grimaldi as a joint enterprise of P.E.A (Rome) and Les Artistes Associés (Paris), *Last Tango in Paris* ran into problems as soon as it was shown to the Italian censors. The film contains explicit scenes of sexual intercourse and when it was viewed in New York by its distributors, United Artists Corporation, they agreed that some editing would be necessary before a general release campaign could be arranged. The film was presented as the closing item at the New York Film Festival on the evening of October 14, 1972, and it was flown in under guard from Rome with provision for a single showing and then returned the next day. Italian law prohibits the showing of an Italian film abroad before it has passed the Italian censors, but an exception was granted, after much discussion, in this instance. *Last Tango in Paris* made a stunning impact on the festival audience in New York; Bertolucci received an ovation but at a party which followed the showing it was evident that the film had disturbed and shocked many of those who had seen it.

The film was ruled not pornographic by an Italian court, and was released commercially in New York on February 1, 1973.

In *Last Tango in Paris* Marlon Brando appears as a middle-aged American—but not the kind of American in Paris glorified by either George Gershwin or Ernest Hemingway. This is a confused, tortured, sexually aggressive expatriate, whose wife has just committed suicide. Eager to escape the dingy hotel in which he lives, he lolates an apartment not far from the Eiffel Tower. Here he comes across a young girl, Jeanne (Maria Schneider), who is also looking over the apartment with the idea of renting it when she marries in a week's time. Jeanne is a modish, lively Parisienne and her fiancé, Tom (Jean-Pierre Léaud), is a documentary moviemaker, who follows her about Paris photographing her as she prepares for the marriage. Fortunately, he does not follow her to the empty apartment. There, within minutes of their meeting, Paul (Brando) seduces Jeanne and embarks on a sexual tryst that lasts for three days. The two know nothing of each other, not even their names. Their affair is a purely physical, isolated experience, and the apartment becomes, as Bertolucci intended, an island on which are examined certain aspects of human relationships, particularly the male, sexual domination of the female.

The film is both intensely erotic and intensely realistic, and among the audience at the New York Film Festival there was much speculation that it would probably embarrass and frighten some viewers as much as it would titillate others, not only because of its sexual material but because of its searing exploration of values and attitudes. Bertolucci wrote the screenplay in collaboration with his editor, Franco Arcalli, but in probing the American psyche Bertolucci sought, and received, the rapport and help of Brando. Some directors have been driven almost to distraction by Brando's work methods, his hesitant, questing approach to his material. But in this case it was exactly what the director wanted. Bertolucci had prepared a detailed script with full dialogue, but he laid it aside whenever Brando wanted to bring his own interpretation to the part. Bertolucci was stimulated by the actor's constant questioning of

With Maria Schneider

With Maria Schneider

lines and motives, and he feels that his association with Brando has furthered his understanding of film making, particularly as it applies to the revealing of human nature.

Among those present at the New York Film Festival showing of *Last Tango in Paris* was Pauline Kael, who shortly thereafter wrote an extended review for *The New Yorker*,* in which she described it as the film that had made the strongest impression on her in twenty years of film reviewing. Miss Kael has on previous occasions expressed admiration for Brando, for his ability to draw directly from life and from himself. In reviewing this film Miss Kael offers a personal recollection of a young Brando and a reflection on an ability that is of the rarest:

We all know that movie actors often merge with their roles in a way that stage actors don't, quite, but Brando did it even on the stage. I was in New York when he played his famous small role in *Truckline Cafe* in 1946; arriving late at a performance, and seated in the center of the second row, I looked up and saw what I thought was an actor having a seizure onstage. Embarrassed for him, I lowered my eyes, and it wasn't until the young man who'd brought me grabbed my arm and said, "Watch this guy!" that I realized he was *acting.* I think a lot of people will make my old mistake when they see Brando's performance as Paul; I think some may prefer to make this mistake, so they won't have to recognize how deep he goes and what he dredges up. Expressing a character's sexuality makes new demands on an actor, and Brando has no trick accent to play with this time, and no putty on his face. It's perfectly apparent that the role was conceived for Brando, using elements of his past as integral parts of the character. Bertolucci wasn't surprised by what Brando did; he was ready to use what Brando brought to the role. And when Brando is a full creative presence on the screen, the realism transcends the simulated actuality of any known style of *cinéma vérité,* because his surface accuracy expresses what's going on underneath. He's an actor; when he shows you something, he lets you know what it means.

* *The New Yorker*, October 28, 1972.

With Maria Schneider

With director Bernardo Bertolucci

AFTERWORD: The Oscar

To the surprise of almost no one, Marlon Brando was awarded the Oscar at the Academy Awards presentation in Los Angeles on the evening of March 27, 1973, as Best Actor of the previous year for his portrayal of Don Vito Corleone in *The Godfather*. Due to the great success of the film and the publicity given Brando for both this picture and *The Last Tango in Paris*, the odds were heavily in favor that he would win. And like so many of the top Oscars there was an emotional factor involved, in the case of Brando a sense of re-affirmation of an admittedly great but wayward actor who had become alienated by, or with, Hollywood. Be that as it may, it was a "welcome home" extended to an actor in no way concerned with being welcomed home.

Brando had rejected the award offered him by the Hollywood Foreign Press Association and he made the same decision with The Academy of Motion Picture Arts and Sciences. An uproar of applause greeted his name as he was announced Best Actor, but instead of Brando, an attractive Indian girl named Shasheen Littlefeather proceeded to the podium. Miss Littlefeather, an Apache member of the Native American Affirmative Image Committee, spoke for Brando and declared his rejection as a protest against the film industry's depiction of the Indian as a villain in movies. Her short speech invited a few boos and derisive cries from some of the audience, but Miss Littlefeather maintained a dignity that drew respect and she was applauded as she left the stage. She carried a written statement from Brando, reading a fraction of it to the audience but afterwards releasing the whole to the press.

Most of Brando's six-hundred-word statement decried the treatment given American Indians throughout the history of the United States but it also touched upon the grievances of foreign policy: "So I, as a member in this profession, do not feel that I can as a citizen of the United States accept an award here tonight. I think awards in this country at this time are inappropriate to be received or given until the condition of the American Indian is drastically altered. If we are not our brother's keeper, at least let us not be his executioner."

Brando's gesture was not received without criticism. Some felt that a better impression might have been made by his having the Indian girl accept the Oscar in the name of brotherhood, and others believed he would have made greater impact by rejecting the award in person. Brando explained his absence by saying he was at the time on his way to Wounded Knee, South Dakota, to support the Oglala Sioux in their militant protest against job and racial discrimination. Brando's action was but a minor surprise to those who have worked with him in films, those who have long known him to be unconventional, unpredictable and completely individual. One such person at the Academy Awards presentation neatly summed up the feelings of the industry when he shrugged his shoulders, gave a wry smile and said, "Well, Marlon's done it again."